PREACHING
FOR OUR PLANET

MOWBRAY PREACHING SERIES

Series editor: D. W. Cleverley Ford

Preaching the Risen Christ: D. W. Cleverley Ford
Preaching through the Acts of the Apostles: D. W. Cleverley Ford
Preaching through the Life of Christ: D. W. Cleverley Ford
Preaching through the Prophets: John B. Taylor
Preaching through Saint Paul: Derrick Greeves
More Preaching from the New Testament: D. W. Cleverley Ford
Preaching on Devotional Occasions: D. W. Cleverley Ford
More Preaching on Favourite Hymns: Frank Colquhoun
Preaching on Special Occasions, Volume 3: Edward H. Patey
Preaching on Great Themes: D. W. Cleverley Ford
Preaching on the Holy Spirit: D. W. Cleverley Ford
Preaching on the Lord's Supper: Encounter with Christ: Ian
   MacLeod
Preaching on Prayer: Monica Ditmas
Preaching the Incarnate Christ: D. W. Cleverley Ford
Preaching for Our Planet: Hugh Montefiore

Preaching through the Christian Year Volume 12: John M. Turner

Preaching at the Parish Communion:
   ASB Epistles – Sundays: Year One, Volume 2: Dennis Runcorn
   ASB Epistles – Sundays: Year Two, Volume 2: John Vipond
   ASB Gospels – Sundays: Year One: Dennis Runcorn
   ASB Gospels – Sundays: Year One, Volume 2: Eric Devenport
   ASB Gospels – Sundays: Year Two, Volume 2: Peter Morris

PREACHING
FOR OUR PLANET

HUGH MONTEFIORE

MOWBRAY

Mowbray
A Cassell imprint
Villiers House, 41/47 Strand, London WC2N 5JE, England
387 Park Avenue South, New York, NY 10016–8810, USA

First published 1992

British Library Cataloguing-in-Publication Data
A catalogue record for this book is available from the British Library.

ISBN 0-264-67281-X

Phototypeset by Intype, London
Printed and bound in Great Britain by
Biddles Ltd, Guildford and King's Lynn

CONTENTS

FOREWORD

For many generations, the human exploitation of renewable resources in agriculture, fisheries, forestry and wildlife remained in general balance with the ability of the earth's natural regenerative systems. Only about 200 years ago the human population started to explode, first in the industrialized countries and then in the less prosperous countries of Asia, Africa and Latin America. More people need more resources and richer people consume more as individuals. The earth has now reached a situation where it can no longer sustain the ever-increasing demands and pressures of its human inhabitants.

Similar crises have struck individual civilizations throughout history and their legacy is eroded treeless hills, deserts or jungles, but this is the first time that over-exploitation has occurred on a global scale. It is this new dimension to an old problem which has posed such a dilemma for all the world's great religions. The writers of the Scriptures and the Church Fathers were not confronted with such a stark situation in their time, and therefore they did not have much to say about the conservation of the natural environment and its resources.

This means that Christians today have a duty to think through their attitude to the whole of God's creation, and to be clear about the principles which they believe should guide their conduct. This is a contemporary issue and a challenge to the contemporary Church, and Bishop Montefiore is to be congratulated on tackling some of these very thorny problems.

INTRODUCTION

These sermons are intended for the ordinary churchgoer who has no particular knowledge of environmental matters and their importance for today, but would like to think about them within the perspective of his or her Christian faith.

I have avoided wherever possible the use of technical terms, but, when they have had to be used, I have tried to include explanations. I have also attempted to dispense with statistics whenever I can. A sermon format precludes the use of notes to verify the many statements that I make. I have used a wide variety of sources, but I am particularly grateful for information from the Friends of the Earth and from the Worldwatch Institute in Washington, DC.

Readers who may wish to take the matters further will find the following books useful:

The Gaia Atlas of Planet Management, ed. N. Myers (Pan Books, 1985);
This Common Inheritance (Cm 1200; HMSO, 1990);
The State of the Environment (OECD, Paris 1991);
State of the World (Worldwatch Institute Annual Report; Norton, USA);
Gaia: The Practical Science of Planetary Medicine, James Lovelock (Gaia Books, 1991);
Save the Planet, Jonathon Porritt (Dorling Kindersley, 1991).

I am grateful to Canon Douglas Cleverley Ford for his wise and helpful comments.

3 September 1991   HUGH MONTEFIORE

1
CREATION

The earth is the Lord's, and the fullness thereof . . .
PSALM 24.1 (AV)

Nowadays everyone seems to be concerned about the environment. It's not in itself a very beautiful word, and a few years ago we hardly ever heard it, but nowadays it is on everybody's lips. Supermarkets sell products which they call 'environmentally friendly'. Voluntary organizations for the conservation of the environment abound. The Friends of the Earth has over 200,000 members and the figure is still rising. Greenpeace and the World Wide Fund for Nature raise large sums of money every year to spend on campaigning and education. University departments now devote themselves to different aspects of the environment. Even a new kind of discipline, called 'environmental economics', has emerged. These are all secular organizations or institutions. But ought the Christian Church to be interested and ought individual Christians to be concerned?

A PROPER CONCERN FOR THE CHURCH

At first sight it might seem that the answer is 'No'. It could be said that when the Christian Church speaks out about the environment, it is merely climbing on to a secular bandwagon. Christians, we might say, should be concerned about the spiritual life. Environmental concern seems to be a modern version of the secular idea of 'progress'. Christians, instead of being preoccupied with their souls and with their ultimate destination, which is eternal life with God in heaven, could be accused of switching their attention instead to the things of this world, intent on the kind of sustainable development that will bring more and more of the world's goodies to more and more people. To use a long theological word, they would be engaged in secular eschatology.

But this is to misrepresent why Christians have at last woken up to the fact that they certainly ought to be concerned with the

1

environment. There are even secular environmentalists who accuse the Church of having been the main cause of our waste of non-renewable resources and pollution of the environment. It is a false accusation, but, like many such false accusations, it contains within it a grain of truth. There have been Christians, for example, who have thought that the natural world has been contaminated by original sin and has become so evil that it does not matter what we do with it. But such people have always been the exception rather than the rule. The great majority have known that 'the heavens declare the glory of God, and the firmament showeth his handiwork'. They have been taught by the Scriptures to reverence the works of creation. But it never occurred to them (or indeed to anyone) that the riches of this world were exhaustible, and that pollution could be caused on a national and international scale. It is only recently that human beings have devised the technology which enables them to create these disastrous worldwide effects.

ONLY GOD FULLY UNDERSTANDS THE WORLD

If we look at the Scriptures we find plenty of evidence that 'the earth is the Lord's, and the fullness thereof'. The Book of Job contains some glorious poetry about the work of God in creation when God answered Job out of the whirlwind:

Where wast thou when I laid the foundations of the earth? declare, if thou hast understanding.

Who hath laid the measures thereof, if thou knowest? or who hath stretched the line upon it?

Whereupon are the foundations thereof fastened? or who laid the corner stone thereof;

When the morning stars sang together, and all the sons of God shouted for joy?

Or who shut up the sea with doors, when it brake forth, as if it had issued out of the womb?

When I made the cloud the garment thereof, and thick darkness a swaddlingband for it. . . . (Job 38.4–9)

Hast thou entered into the treasures of the snow? or hast thou seen the treasures of the hail,

Which I have reserved against the time of trouble, against the day of battle and war? (Job 38.22–23)

2

It is hardly surprising that, when confronted with all that and much more besides, Job responded with the words: 'What shall I answer thee? I will lay mine hand upon my mouth' (Job 40.4). You might think that today things are very different: we do know how the planet formed out of the debris of an exploding supernova, how the oceans formed out of hydrogen and oxygen, how the tectonic plates regulate the continents, and how rain, snow and hail come into being. Yes, we know *how* these things happen, but we have not the slightest idea *why* they actually happen. They depend on the so-called 'constants of nature' – and no scientist can tell you why these are as they are. And as for the rain and the snow and the hail, contemporary 'chaos theory' tells us of the so-called 'butterfly effect', so that we can never predict with absolute accuracy, because the smallest effect many thousands of miles away, even a butterfly, can have such escalating results that they are literally unpredictable. It is gloriously true that 'the earth is the Lord's, and the fullness thereof' and only God fully understands it.

THE CREATION IS VAST, BUT GOD IS SOVEREIGN OVER ALL

The prophet Isaiah also spoke movingly about the sovereignty of God over all creation:

Have ye not known? have ye not heard? hath it not been told you from the beginning? have ye not understood from the foundations of the earth?

It is he that sitteth upon the circle of the earth, and the inhabitants thereof are as grasshoppers; that stretcheth out the heavens as a curtain, and spreadeth them out as a tent to dwell in. . . .

To whom then will ye liken me, or shall I be equal? saith the Holy One.

Lift up your eyes on high, and behold who hath created these things, that bringeth out their host by number: he calleth them all by names by the greatness of his might, for that he is strong in power; not one faileth. . . .

Hast thou not known? hast thou not heard, that the everlasting God, the Lord, the Creator of the ends of the earth, fainteth not, neither is weary? there is no searching of his understanding. (Isaiah 40.21–22, 25–26, 28)

The panorama of the universe which is known to us today is even greater than that which Isaiah portrayed. Indeed, it is so vast that we cannot even be sure whether or not it is infinite. Compared with the size of the cosmos and the length of time since the Big Bang, we are nothing like as big as grasshoppers – we are not even the size of a bacterium! We now have sufficient knowledge for scientists to calculate what happened right back to the first few minutes of creation. Some have even surmised that creation came into being as a quantum variation in a vacuum, which increased exponentially, and then, as a result of supercooling – all within the merest fraction of a second – came the Big Bang out of which everything else has emerged, with hundred of millions of galaxies each with billions of stars in various states of development spaced out over billions of 'light years' (the distance that light can travel in a year). These scientists may be right, although there can, by the nature of the case, be no proof. After all, the creation had to come about in some way or other. What they have to explain is why the initial states and the constants of nature that emerged from the Big Bang are just right to give birth to our universe, and if they had been only infinitesimally different, there would not be a universe at all. Perhaps we are surrounded by countless numbers of invisible 'failed' universes, and ours is the one which had the right characteristics to make good. How can we know? What we can say is that, while our faith is in no way dependent on what the scientists tell us about creation, it is entirely consistent with it. That holds good for the universe as a whole, and particularly for our little planet Earth, where even more amazing coincidences have resulted in the emergence and evolution of life. 'The earth is the Lord's, and the fullness thereof.'

GOD CREATED THE EARTH AND ITS FULLNESS FOR ITS OWN SAKE

The Scriptures tell us God did not merely create the world for our sakes: he takes pleasure in Leviathan, and in making flowers spring up in the wilderness where no human being has trod. It is in particular to chapter 1 of Genesis that we turn when we want to find out the Jewish picture of creation which Jesus, as a good Jew, naturally took for granted. In fact, this chapter is a reworking of the old Babylonian creation-myth of Marduk, suitably adapted to the monotheistic faith of Jews. This in itself should tell us a great deal: we are acting biblically if we take the creation stories of our day – and today these are scientific – so long as we suitably adapt them to our Trinitarian faith in God the Father who is the Creator, God the Son who is the Logos or meaning behind creation, and God the Holy Spirit who is personally immanent within it. The first chapter of Genesis is not meant to be a scientific treatise, and we abuse it if we try to fit the Seven Days of creation into our present knowledge of evolution. But it is inspired because it tells us fundamental spiritual truths: that God alone is the Creator who, by his Word, causes things to be in an orderly manner. At his Word the oceans 'bring forth' moving creatures that have life, and flying fowl, and on land Mother Earth 'brings forth' living creatures after their kind – beasts and creeping things and finally human beings. 'The earth is the Lord's and the fullness thereof.'

Men and women are the crown of creation, being made in the image of God. But humanity is only part of creation and needs to play its part within the whole drama of living things. This is wonderfully portrayed in Psalm 104, where we have an inspired meditation on the power and the providence of God in his created world. True, God created herbs for the service of humanity, and wine that makes glad our hearts. But the trees and the birds and the wild goats and conies and young lions all have their place for their own sake; and as for human beings, we are merely told that 'Man goeth forth unto his work and to his labour until the evening' (Psalm 104.23). Rightly the Psalmist comments: 'O Lord, how manifold are thy works! In wisdom hast thou made them all: the earth is full of thy riches' (verse 24).

Perhaps we would not today wish to endorse *all* of creation: the *spirochaeta pallida* which causes syphilis, or the HIV virus which causes AIDS. No doubt the ancient Jews, without guns or other similar deadly devices with which to quell wild animals, may have felt the same about the lion and the adder. The fact is that God has given his creation freedom to develop, and the good far outweighs that which has evil effects. God is the Creator of all that is, and there is none other. And so we say with grateful conviction, 'The earth is the Lord's, and the fullness thereof', and we bow our heads in wonder and worship of the God under whose providence creation has evolved.

2

STEWARDSHIP

. . . Who then is that faithful and wise steward, whom his lord shall make ruler over his household?

LUKE 12.42 (AV)

THE PROCREATION OF A CHILD

When two parents look for the first time on their new-born baby, they are lost in amazement. How on earth did they make this little bundle of perfection? Of course they know something about the way that it came into being; but it is extraordinary how this tiny human creature, with its right number of toes and fingers and all the thousands of perfectly formed and amazingly complex mechanisms of the human body, can possibly have evolved from such a simple beginning. More than that, this small human being, who has only just seen the light of day, already has the gift of consciousness; and they know that, with their help and care, the baby will grow up with all the sensibilities and feelings as well as the articulateness and reasoning powers of an adult person. What is more, the baby contains part of their very selves; for they have given it the genes which have made it what it will become. They feel bonded to their baby in love, so that they will keep it from harm, and surround it with their affection and love.

We speak of procreating a child, and we use that word because there is some similarity between the act of a parent in creating a child, and the act of our heavenly Father in bringing the universe into being. Of course there are differences as well as similarities. In the first place, a parent does not actually create a child from nothing, as God has created the universe from a vacuum, but a human life is built up from already existing substances. Wonderful as the mystery of the developing child is, it is as nothing in comparison with the wonder of the developing universe. It is vaster than we can imagine, greater than we can comprehend. Just because of that, and because we live on this planet, we tend to concentrate our attention on that small part of God's creation that we actually know on earth. Here we glimpse something of the marvellous richness of God's creation and, when we think

6

of the development of all this complexity and beauty, we are lost in the same kind of amazement and admiration as are the parents of a new-born child.

GOD CREATES OUT OF NOTHING

Can we find a picture of God in creation which is closer to reality than that of the procreation of a child? I think we can – when we think of a poet or dramatist who creates a book or a play. He creates a whole world out of nothing. Without his imagination and application, it would not have come into being. He creates people, and the people have characters of their own, indeed lives of their own, and he cannot make them do things out of keeping with their characters (or, if he does, he is a bad writer). He not only creates people, he creates the whole world in which they live. But although the people he creates and the world around them have lives of their own, at the same time there is something of the author in them all. He has created them, and in his imagination they live and move and have their being. Furthermore, although the people 'do their own thing' in the story or the drama, the author exercises an overall control. They only exist, as it were, within his providential care; and if things seem to be getting out of hand, so that the plot is disrupted, the author introduces some way of bringing it back to where it should be. So the author is not only the creator; he is not only immanent in his creation, but in a sense he is at work to redeem the story if need be from going wrong. When the author has finished his work, he too wants to cry out, 'Behold, it is very good'.

No analogy can be adequate for the wonderful work of God in creation, but these examples can perhaps help us to glimpse at what divine creation means. It is not only that God has created everything out of nothing – or out of the Big Bang, as we perhaps would prefer to put it today – and 'Behold it is very good'. It is also that his Spirit is to be found within it, so that the evolution of the universe, and that of course includes the Milky Way and the solar system and Planet Earth, are all within his providential care, as well as the billions of individual human beings living on our planet. And he is at work to help to put things right when they go wrong, to bring the process back to the direction in which it should go, despite many false starts and cul-de-sacs. We must not think of God as setting up the universe like some kind of gigantic machine, and leaving it alone to develop totally under its own momentum. We do not believe in that kind of unapproachable

7

supermonarch. We believe in the Triune God, the Father, Son and Holy Spirit at work throughout his universe in the work of creation, redemption and sanctification.

THE CREATION OF HUMAN BEINGS

Here, on this tiny planet circling round a second-generation middle-aged star which we call the Sun, by some marvel of God's contriving, circumstances were just right for life to have emerged – and not only just right *then*, but a wonderful system of feedback and self-regulation has kept conditions comfortable for the development of life over the whole of the last 4 billion years since life first appeared. We have no means of knowing whether this is the only place in the universe where this has happened. Scientists learned in such matters have calculated that it is probable that life exists somewhere else as well. What we do know is that the emergence of life would be very, very rare, and thus life is very, very precious. Again, we cannot know all of what God's purposes would have been in creating a universe: but we do know one of them. Out of the evolutionary process on this planet there emerged *Homo sapiens*, human beings, capable of thinking and speaking, capable of making choices, of passing moral judgements and of showing spiritual insight, and above all, capable of responding to God's love. His gracious purpose is that intelligent beings should share that love with him for all eternity. We speak of human beings as 'made in God's image' because their special characteristics give them some points of resemblance to God himself, which make them capable of fellowship and communion with him. To say this is in no way to diminish the intrinsic value of all creation or the invaluable function of both living things and inorganic matter in maintaining the stability of Planet Earth.

STEWARDSHIP

If human beings are like God, they ought to behave in a responsible and godlike manner, and co-operate with God. If God is Creator, they must be co-creators of the world he has made. If God is Redeemer, they must be co-redeemers of the world they have spoilt. If God is Sanctifier, they must acknowledge his sanctification of matter everywhere in his universe.

The two stories of creation in chapters 1 and 2 of Genesis are not scientific accounts of how things came into being, but they contain wonderfully inspired insights into God's purpose for man. According to the account in Genesis chapter 2, Adam and Eve were put in charge of nature, in the form of a garden, to use it, enjoy it and care for it. They were accountable to God for the garden: they were its stewards, and the care of the garden was their work of stewardship. Their primal sin was to abuse the natural law which they had been commanded to keep – after that, everything went wrong. But because they now knew good and evil, there was the possibility in the end of a greater good, as their powers expanded. But there was also the possibility of a greater evil.

Jesus teaches a great deal about stewardship. In his parables and sayings on human beings as stewards, he always refers to their accountability to God in their stewardship. 'Who then is that faithful and wise steward, whom his lord shall make ruler over his household?' Human beings are stewards over the whole household of God; that is, over all that is on the earth. In some ways, perhaps the word 'caretaker' might be preferable to 'steward', because a steward is often given absolute power. Our job is not to manage the ecology of the world – that is far too complex – but to take care of it. It is a pity that the Church has taken over the word 'stewardship' to refer to the giving of money. The idea of stewardship really begins in Genesis, with care for the environment, and it is enlarged by Jesus to refer to our stewardship over the whole world. It is all the more necessary to us to remember this because our powers have so greatly increased: our power to do good and our power to inflict evil. Now we are called not only to be co-creators of the natural world, but also co-redeemers, putting right what we have done amiss. We must acknowledge too the sanctification of matter and respect it, for 'behold, it is very good'.

There is always a danger that stewardship can become a means by which the wealthy take it out on the poor. For example, wealthy countries, which first established their position by warships built with wood from their forests, may try to prevent poorer countries today from improving *their* position by selling the products of their tropical rain forests; or again, the wealthy – who can afford to buy free range eggs and chickens – may try to prevent these goods remaining within reach of the less well-off through modern techniques of mass production. It was Anthony Crosland, Secretary of State for the Environment in a Labour government, who described conservation measures as a means by which the rich pull up the ladder behind them. So long as the market is the sole determinant of where foodstuffs go, this danger is always with us. It needs to be guarded against; but it in no way constitutes a decisive argument, since we are concerned with preserving resources and amenities for future generations. We must not 'pull up the ladder' so as to deprive posterity of what we already enjoy.

In 1990, for the first time the British government issued a White Paper on the Environment, *Our Common Inheritance*. I quote from it: 'The starting point for this Government is the ethical imperative of stewardship which must underlie all Government policies'. It reminds us that we do not hold a freehold on our world, only a full repairing lease. Stewardship implies accountability, and a repairing lease implies a landlord. The White Paper speaks of stewardship, but it is not the slightest bit interested in the person to whom humanity is accountable for that stewardship.

There is only one possible person, and that of course is God.

3

ANIMALS AND HUMANS

Are not two sparrows sold for a penny? And not one of them will fall to the ground without your Father's will.

MATTHEW 10.29 (RSV)

The television set has brought us into close contact with the animal world in an astonishing way. We can now see very many species of birds and beasts and reptiles and insects from all over the world which could never have been seen before; and we can see them in their natural habitats. These programmes are rightly very popular. We are struck by the vivid colours and natural beauty of the animals, and by their strangeness, and of course by their tremendous variety. At the same time, there is growing up a new awareness of the way in which we tend to treat animals, and some people have become very strident on their behalf. What are Christians to believe about humanity's relationship to the animal kingdom? This sermon is an attempt to ask that question, and also to gain some answers.

THE TEACHING OF JESUS

Jesus is reported to have said, in the words of my text: 'Are not two sparrows sold for a penny? And not one of them will fall to the ground without your Father's will' – and then he went on to say: 'You are of more value than many sparrows'. This is, I think, one of only three recorded sayings of our Lord about the animal world, and so it makes a good place at which to start. First, he is telling us that human beings are of more value than animals. In the old days this would have been taken for granted, but today there are those who deny it. At the same time, Jesus is saying that even a small bird, which in terms of money is regarded as of minimal value, is still within the range of divine providence. It has intrinsic value in the eyes of God.

THE TEACHING OF THE OLD TESTAMENT

If we want to understand Jesus' view on animals, of course we must go to the Old Testament, which was his Bible. We must return to those early chapters of Genesis. There in chapter 1 we have the days of creation. Human beings and animals were created on the same day, which implies a certain kinship between them, although at the same time there is a difference, because humans were made in the image of God. God tells Adam: '. . . have dominion over the fish of the sea, and over the birds of the air, and over the cattle, and over all the earth, and over every creeping thing that creeps upon the earth' (Genesis 1.26 RSV). Humanity is master. Of course in those early days when Genesis was written, it did not always seem like that. Wild beasts could be very dangerous. Humanity's hold on life was still somewhat precarious. Nonetheless, men and women were on top. The passage does not tell us how humankind is to behave towards the animal kingdom; it simply tells us what we know to be the case – that human beings are dominant and animals are in their power.

In chapter 2 of Genesis there is a different story of creation. According to this account, Adam was created, and God saw that it was not good for him to be alone. So the animals were created, not for his use, but to be his companions, but not on quite the same level as man, because when God created them he brought them before Adam to name them – and to give a name to someone or something denoted authority over them. But the animals did not give Adam sufficient companionship, for they were different; and so we have the story of Eve being formed from Adam's rib, bone of his bone and flesh of his flesh. Of course these are stories, not historical accounts; but they are inspired stories, and they speak to us of deep religious truths. We have noted how they account for the kinship we have with animals and of our mastery over them. I am sure that all of us have felt this kinship with animals. We like their company, we are grateful for their co-operation, we can feel sympathy with them when they suffer, and even moral outrage if they are harmed. At the same time, we exercise mastery over them increasingly as more areas of the globe are brought under man's direct control.

We find elsewhere in the Scriptures corroboration of this attitude towards animals. It was not only humanity that was saved at the flood, but God had mercy on every species of animal too, because he valued them: they all went into the ark. God delights in animals, as we are told he delighted in Leviathan the sea monster; and at the end of the book of Job we are given wonderful descriptions of animals, especially the horse and the crocodile, as examples of God's creation. There is companionship too between animal and human, as in the quaint story of Balaam and his ass. Psalm 104 gives us a marvellous rundown of the animal creation, with humans simply appearing at the end of the list. There are injunctions not to cause unnecessary suffering, for example in taking fledglings from a bird's nest, and 'a righteous man has regard to the life of his beast'. In the Wisdom literature, moral lessons are drawn from animal behaviour; and even in the Prophets we are told of animals who obey their natural law, while humans do not: 'The stork in the heavens knoweth her appointed times, and the turtle and the crane and the swallow observe the time of their coming; but my people know not the judgement of the Lord' (Jeremiah 8.7).

RESPECT FOR THE ANIMAL CREATION

Yet humans are masters of the animal kingdom, because man and woman are made in the image of God. They alone can articulate and think on a high level, and they alone can communicate with God and their fellows in language. They alone are capable of moral behaviour, and they have in the light of these endowments developed their cultural life and achieved mastery over the animals. Because they are made in the image of God, they are under obligation to exercise that mastery in a godlike way, by showing respect for the animal creation and acting in a responsible manner.

Admittedly we now know that the human/animal divide is not as wide as we used to think. Animals can communicate with each other by sign language, or by sound or by ultrasonics. Chimpanzees can count, and baboons can practise deliberate deceit. Nonetheless, there is still a divide, and human beings alone can communicate with God. They are accountable to God for the way in which they treat animals. They are stewards of the animal creation – almost, one might say, priests of the natural world, representing the animals before God, and under an obligation to act in a godlike manner towards them. Although it is popular nowadays to speak of animal rights, it is hardly correct, for there can be no rights without corresponding duties, and animals have no moral sense. But *we* have duties towards animals. We must treat them with respect because they have value in God's eyes. We must avoid animal suffering, so far as we can, because it is always morally wrong to cause unnecessary suffering to those within our power. If we keep them in captivity, we must avoid gross overcrowding and permit them to perform their basic natural functions, like grooming and lying down and having space to exercise their limbs.

13

They should have freedom of association with other animals, facilities for bodily care such as rest and sleep, proper food and drink to maintain full health, opportunity for exploration and play, especially if they are young, and the satisfaction of their minimal territorial requirements.

There are many difficult moral issues to be faced over our dealings with animals. These include fishing and blood sports, the domestication of wild animals so as to farm them for food, the wearing of animal furs and skins, their use in testing drugs and toiletries, their retention in zoos and their domestication as pets for the pleasure of their owners. I want now however to major on just one basic question: is it right to kill animals? According to the stories in Genesis, when humans and animals were created, no licence was given to humanity to kill them. According to Genesis, the animals had grass, and humankind had grain and fruit on which to live, so humans were vegetarians. After the wickedness which led to the Flood, however, this rule in our fallen world is relaxed. 'Every moving thing that liveth shall be meat for you; even as the green herb have I given you all things' (Genesis 9.3). And as a result, Noah and his sons are told, '. . . the fear of you and the dread of you shall be upon every beast of the earth, and upon every fowl of the air, upon all that moveth upon the earth, and upon all the fishes of the sea; into your hand are they delivered' (Genesis 9.2). Enmity has taken the place of companionship and, apart from domesticated animals, this enmity is still clearly to be seen.

These are stories, not accurate accounts of prehistory. But they contain spiritual truths. In the world of paradise human beings and animals are companions to one another. As Isaiah puts it as he looks forward to Paradise Regained:

> And the cow and the bear shall feed; their young ones shall lie down together: and the lion shall eat straw like the ox. And the sucking child shall play on the hole of the asp, and the weaned child shall put his hand on the cockatrice's den. They shall not hurt nor destroy in all my holy mountain . . . (Isaiah 11.7–9)

People are vegetarians for a variety of reasons, but Christians cannot regard them as oddballs if they take their Scriptures seriously. St Paul recognized this, although he wrote to the Romans about those who eat herbs as 'weak in the faith'. But he may have meant here those who still felt bound to keep Jewish food taboos rather than those who were outright vegetarians.

At the same time we are licensed to eat animals for food, a practice that is built into our genes from our animal past as primates, just as our love of nuts and fruits also belongs to the time when our prehuman forebears lived in the trees on a vegetarian diet. If we do eat animals, we ought to see that they are kept in a way which maintains their respect, and that they are humanely slaughtered.

ENDANGERED SPECIES

However, the scale of our human activity is such that we do not merely endanger particular animals but whole species. There are 1,390,902 known species in the world today, with a conservative estimate of the *total* number of species reckoned at 10 million! We all know about the danger to certain types of whale or to the giant panda, but we may not realize that on present reckoning a fifth of all species will have been exterminated by the end of the century – and this does not take account of possible global warming. Mammals account for only 0.3 per cent of the planet's population, but this extermination of these species will have been accomplished purely by *Homo sapiens*.

Of course there is a natural rise and fall of different species, and in the distant past there have been mass exterminations. But for us to exterminate all these species is to destroy the wonderful variety of life that has under God's providence taken millions of years to evolve; and it must be wrong. Is there ever a justification for the extinction of a species? Only very occasionally. If humankind has been given 'dominion' over all living things, human beings are surely justified in eliminating species which can be shown to be both inimical to and parasitic on mankind. For example, the world would be a better place if the HIV virus (which gives rise to AIDS) could be eliminated as we hope the smallpox virus already has been.

As human beings we are dominant, but we must treat animals with respect, and if we do have to kill them we must not cause unnecessary suffering. The preservation of whole species deserves special care, for they cannot be re-created. It is impossible to lay down rules which meet every case, but we must see the animal creation as within the providence of God and carrying out vital functions in maintaining the stability of Planet Earth. We must act in so far as we may in a godlike way towards the animal kingdom. But I am sure that you will agree that it is a terrible indictment on the human race that we have already exterminated so many species of living things that have taken so long to evolve. It shows contempt for the wealth and variety of God's creation. What can we do about it? There are plenty of voluntary organizations which set out to protect endangered species and to prevent even more being exterminated, if we wish to support them.

4

WORLD POPULATION

*And God blessed them, and God said unto them, Be fruitful, and
multiply . . .*
GENESIS 1.28 (AV)

THE INSTINCT TO REPRODUCE

Do you remember, at the last christening you attended, how delighted
everyone was at the birth of the baby? It is almost always the case.
Everyone with children has experienced for himself or herself that
blessing on fertility which God, according to Genesis, pronounced on
Adam and Eve. The baby will cause a lot of hard work for the mother,
but when it is born she will be delighted. The baby may strain family
resources, but father is also pleased. So are the friends and relations.
A baby is almost always a source for thanksgiving, even if in some
more primitive societies this is somewhat muted when the baby is a
girl, which is of course bound to be the case in just over 50 per cent of
all births. This urge to reproduce is at the root of a very high proportion of all animal activities. It lies, of course, behind their urge to
mate. It lies behind the contests between males to secure the best
mate; and a great deal of time and trouble is spent on feeding, protecting and educating the young. With human beings the urge to found a
family is equally strong, although often unacknowledged. Those
women who beautify and groom themselves in order to appear attrac-
tive do so, often unconsciously, to attract a mate and so found a
family. Males who chase girls are motivated by the same urge. Human
bodies, male and female, are shaped differently. This is to fit them
for their different but complementary roles in producing, rearing,
protecting and feeding the family. The fact that young humans take a
proportionately longer time to mature than the young of other species
means that human parents have to spend a large percentage of their
lives in caring for their children.

THE MEANING BEHIND THE GENESIS TEXT

At first sight the command in Genesis seems to license an ever-increasing population. 'Be fruitful, and multiply' is pronounced unconditionally. Yet the order was given to 'replenish the earth', not to overfill it. 'Replenish' suggests that without such a command there would be the danger that the human race could not sustain itself. And indeed that was the case. In prehistoric times the expectation of life was very short. Most children would not have survived until the age of puberty, and so they could not have reproduced. Illness took its toll. Primitive people lacked our resources against natural disasters. Hunger and the lack of the right nourishment would have resulted in a lack of immunity against infections. Human beings had dominion over nature, but at times it was a somewhat uncertain dominion, and sometimes it was animals rather than humans that survived an encounter. If families had not been large, they would not have survived at all.

TODAY'S POPULATION TRENDS

Today in the developed world the average size of a family has dramatically decreased until, in many cases, the number of births in a country roughly equals the number of deaths; and in some cases the number of new births is actually below replacement level. A drop in fertility levels is not confined to such countries though. Some developing countries (if we may count Hong Kong and China among them) have reduced the rate of population growth spectacularly as a result of exceptional measures by their governments in the way of disincentives. But in most Third World countries the rate of births still far outstrips the rate of deaths, and so their populations are continuing to increase, although not always at the exponential rates of the earlier years of this century. Kenya is at the top of the table, with an average of eight children for every woman in the land.

In all countries people may expect to live longer than in the past; and even if only four of those eight children for each Kenyan woman lived long enough to reproduce themselves, and four of their eight children did the same, within three generations there would be sixteen citizens instead of the original two grandparents – that is what the population explosion is all about! Today there are 5.3 billion people on earth, and it is expected that by the year 2025 – not much more than thirty years from now – there will be at least 8.5 billion. Think of the colossal drain on resources! We have nowadays comparatively good death control without the corresponding birth control.

There are many reasons for large families in the Third World. Their people largely live by subsistence farming, and young children constitute unpaid labour for the smallholding. In these countries there are no pension schemes and no free National Health Service, so the more children there are in the family, the greater is the potential support for the parents when they are ill or elderly. Parents expect some of their children to die in infancy, and so they make sure that they will have others to survive them. A large family is a way in which a man proves his virility and a woman her fertility. Many women, however, would prefer smaller families. About a third of the 140 million women who become pregnant every year in the Third World do not want another baby. But they do not have access to contraceptive means that are safe, reliable, within their means and also within their competence. In the old days, a kind of natural contraception was practised, because a mother would breast-feed her children until the age of four; and while she is feeding one child she will be exceedingly unlikely to conceive another. But such habits have tended to die out under the influence of Western customs and Western advertising. Many children have died because their mothers have believed Western advertisements which told them that milk powder would give their baby a better start. But so often this powder is mixed with contaminated water and infants die of gastro-enteritis.

Parents have had large families in the belief that this will help them financially, but in fact the reverse has happened. Populations outstrip the ability of poor countries to feed their people. No doubt to an individual couple there seems no harm in one large family; but when the effects of hundreds of millions of large families are aggregated, the result can be catastrophic. Dr Ehrlich, one of the world's most distinguished ecologists, believes that the world's burgeoning population lies at the root of its environmental crisis. Certainly the population explosion is colossal. Just think of it. In less than 35 years, the world population is expected to increase by 3.2 billion, an increase of over 60 per cent; and, of that increase, 3 billion will come from the Third World. Put it another way. I have been preaching so far for some seven minutes. During that time 1,918 babies will have been born and 679 people will have died – an increase of over 1,200 simply in the seven minutes I have been preaching. This year there are 93 million more people than in the previous year, and even with AIDS the number goes up each year. It is expected that world population will 'stabilize' around 11 or 12 billion sometime in the next century. I don't want to drown you in statistics, but these figures really are stupendous.

POPULATION AND THE ENVIRONMENT

It is wonderful that agriculture has been able so far to keep up. But there is a limit and we are approaching it. We cannot expect the 'technological fix' always to rescue us from our troubles. In 1989, for the first time world population outstripped world cereal output. Admittedly, fighting and unrest, with millions of displaced refugees, have contributed to this imbalance, and of course there is room for improvement in farming practices and in distribution; but aid often discourages local farmers from increasing production, because it reduces the price of locally grown crops. The fact remains that we are reaching a point of no return when yet more terrible famines may be predicted.

It is not just food. Many poor people are pastoralists, because the soil is too poor for crops; and population pressures demand more cattle than the land can stand. There is also an increasing demand for all non-renewable resources, especially for energy. Wood for cooking and heating is in particular demand. Surrounding neighbourhoods are being stripped of brushwood and bushes, and this results in the erosion of the soil, and then climatic changes occur. In the animal kingdom it sometimes happens that as a result of a succession of good breeding years and favourable weather, herds of wild beasts may very greatly increase. But there is a limit imposed by the environment, and when that limit is reached there is often a catastrophic decline as nature ensures that numbers come into balance. This is the kind of situation we may expect to find with human beings. Such a catastrophe would not affect only the countries concerned. We are now all one world. Not only is imported food needed to allay famines, but there is also disruption in trade patterns, and as a result of environmental degradation there would be world climatic changes.

REMEDIES FOR THE SITUATION

It cannot be God's will that we human beings should breed ourselves out of existence. It cannot be God's will that we should exhaust non-renewable resources because of our large families. The Roman Cath-

19

olic Church condemns all forms of artificial contraceptives, and requires each act of intercourse to be open to conception; but lately even Pope John Paul II has admitted (not without understatement) that 'one cannot deny the existence, especially in the southern hemisphere, of a demographic problem which creates difficulties for development'. Way back in 1958 the Lambeth Conference of Anglican Bishops spoke of the need for a wise stewardship of the resources of the family in the regulation of the number of children, and approved artificial contraception in ways mutually agreeable to the couples concerned. We need also to take thought for a wise stewardship of the resources of the whole human family in considering the number of children in each particular family.

The procreation of children is a very intimate matter; and the number of children in a family has to be decided by husband and wife, and not by the state. But it is also a matter with implications for the whole world. The Churches, even though they differ on means of contraception, agree that there is a need to limit the size of families. This applies particularly to the Third World, for elsewhere deaths and births are approximately in balance. It ought to be the rule, in all churches, that the representatives of the Churches, in preparing couples for marriage before their wedding, should emphasize the urgent need to limit families. But it is a difficult matter for the Western world to preach to the developing world on this matter, for this smacks of self-righteousness. Nor is teaching about a wise stewardship before God in deciding family size likely to be really effective. It is the kind of argument which lies beyond the scope of a peasant farmer in deepest Africa. He is unlikely to think in global terms, and in any case he is unlikely to know the facts.

Is there then any real hope of limiting world population increase? When the standard of living of a country increases, and when wealth is more evenly shared, the rate of population growth slows down. Doubtless more could be done by establishing disincentives for large families, but why should fewer resources be available to certain families, none of whose members were in a position to ask to be born? Short of compulsory sterilization (and when India tried that, there was rightly an outcry), it is not possible to achieve population control without the goodwill of parents. How then can we in the West assist, and so remove one of the worst – perhaps *the* worst – sources of environmental degradation? Without doubt, by helping to make available contraceptives to the large number of women in the Third World who want them but cannot get them; and also by helping to raise the standard of living in those countries. Could we not ease Third World debt, encourage investment and agree to transfer technologies? These are not only good in themselves, but will help to stabilize world population.

Have you ever thought of *praying* for these to come to pass?

5

FORESTS

*Open thy doors, O Lebanon, that the fire may devour thy cedars.
Howl, fir tree; for the cedar is fallen; . . . howl, O ye oaks of
Bashan; for the forest of the vintage is come down.*

ZECHARIAH 11.1–2 (AV)

In the ancient world a tall tree like a cedar stood for strength and
power. We find the prophets referring to the great world empires of
Assyria and Egypt as cedars. In the Psalms a good man is compared to
a cedar. Trees were held in honour. When Zechariah wanted to
prophesy of the fall of Lebanon, he spoke of fire devouring its cedars,
like a city that is taken captive and has been set on fire. He felt a sense
of sadness, of pain, of outrage at the destruction of the forests of
Lebanon which were an object of admiration in Old Testament times.

Today the trees of the world are being devoured and felled and
burned – particularly in the great tropical rain forests, but not only
there. They are no longer regarded as natural symbols of strength, for
nowadays we live in an age of man-made concrete and steel, unknown
in the ancient world. Trees are often regarded in economic terms,
valuable for their timber, or as a nuisance, to be cleared and uprooted
so that oil can be extracted from underneath them, or agriculture
practised where once they stood.

THE FUNCTION OF TREES

Yet a tree is so much more than an economic object or a nuisance. It
performs wonderful functions in the world of nature – in some
respects, unique functions. It gives cohesion to the soil, and keeps it
in being. When forests are cut down, the friable soil is quickly open to
erosion, and flash floods can carry it off and form steep gullies and
leave a wilderness. Topsoil which has taken thousands of years to
form can be lost to a future generation.

Again, forests recycle the moisture. They constitute the world's
lungs. A big tree sucks up huge amounts of water from its roots, and

moisture is returned to the air by evapotranspiration through its leaves. Thus clouds form and the moisture is returned to the atmosphere, so that the cycle of life-giving rain is continued. Cut down the forests, and the wind pattern and the rain pattern is altered; and that may also mean a change in the ocean currents, with disastrous results. Tragically enough it is in the tropics that most of the forests are now being cut down, and people by doing this are helping to dig their own graves, for in a short time the pitiless sun will beat down upon a denuded landscape without the life-giving rain that transforms and cools it. Furthermore, the forests provide a canopy for the torrential rainstorms, ensuring that they do not beat down on the ground, but reach it gently through the thick cover that it provides, so that water supplies are conserved. In the same way the canopy absorbs the heat and the light, so that at ground level it is shady and comparatively cool. Again, the forests help to recycle the carbon dioxide in the atmosphere, fixing the carbon in their branches and stems, and releasing the oxygen to purify the air. Chlorophyll is part of God's gracious providence, whereby the atmosphere is kept in a state comfortable for life. At present rates of destruction, 65 per cent of the world's rain forests will have disappeared within ten years. When 70 per cent of an ecosystem disappears, the rest may not be able to survive, with catastrophic results.

You may think that I am exaggerating in speaking in these terms, so let me share with you an experience I have had myself. It was an expedition to the famous rock city of Petra, the capital of the ancient Nabatean Arab people, now situated in Jordan, and probably mentioned in the Old Testament under the name of Selah. The journey there a hundred years ago was through forest country, and the climate was temperate, and there was abundance of flora and fauna. But when I went there it was a bare and barren desert, and blazingly hot. It was hard to believe that there had been such a quick transformation, but all the trees had been cut down to provide fuel for the Turkish railway engines on the line that had been constructed for purposes of war in those parts. The result has been not only to turn the lush countryside from forest to desert, but also to change the climate so that the sun burns down mercilessly on the barren desert. This is a terrible parable of what is going to happen to the tropical areas where the rain forests have been destroyed.

WHAT TREES PROVIDE

Forests provide a way of life for the indigenous people who live in them and respect them. These people are seldom consulted before the trees are felled. And when the trees have been cut down these people have nowhere to go and nothing to do. They are a prey to illnesses against which they have not been able to build up resistance. Sometimes they are deliberately shot, sometimes they just die out. They do not stand a chance. It is not only human beings that are snuffed out. The tropical rain forests cover only about 6 per cent of the world's surface, but they contain about half of all the living species of the world! Many of these are as yet unknown. In the last ten years at least twenty new species of birds have been found in the South American forests alone. Indeed, it is difficult to *prove* that a species is extinct, if only because much of the forest is unexplored. Nonetheless, the International Union for the Conservation of Nature and Natural Resources issues authoritative Red Books of endangered species, with lists of species of mammals and birds endangered or made extinct by logging in the forests.

These forests also contain remarkable plants. Did you know where tomatoes, pineapples, cocoa and rice originally came from? They came from the rain forests. Did you know that the rain forests are an apothecary's treasure trove, that quinine for malaria, curare the muscle relaxant, and vincristine for the treatment of leukaemia are some of the forest's many treasures? That chemicals used for the treatment of bronchitis, laryngitis and epilepsy come from plants found in the rain forests? Did you know that 70 per cent of the plants identified as having anti-cancer properties come from the rain forests? We cannot afford to lose all this bio-diversity. In any case, species have a right to exist for their own sake, and we are not justified in destroying these gifts of God which have taken so many millions of years to evolve.

THE DESTRUCTION OF TREES

However, we must not be too self-righteous about the way in which others destroy these forests. The destruction of forests has been taking place for centuries. If you compare the original forest cover with the present situation of countries outside Europe and the former USSR, for which figures are not available, you will find that a third of the world's forests has disappeared! Much of England was once covered with forests, and so was Wales. Nowadays Sherwood Forest has shrunk dramatically, while the Forest of Arden is almost no more. Spain was once covered with forests, but now the soil is often thin and poor. Before warships were made of metal, they provided an insatiable market for hardwood forest trees. What forests do remain in Europe are today mostly under threat from acid rain, but that is another and different problem. The people of the Third World think it hypocritical of us to complain about their destruction of forests when we have done just the same ourselves. Indonesia, with its plans for 56 new large pulp and paper mills over the next fifteen years, is particularly incensed. Ranching is carried out in areas that have been deforested, especially in South America; and wealthy countries in the developed world buy the cheap and inferior meat that is produced there. It may be in the next beefburger you eat. British firms also have direct interests in these areas. British Gas, for example, owns half a million acres of rain forest in Ecuador, where it has been prospecting for oil. And the British buy the hardwoods that come from the tropical forests. Furthermore, the countries which possess these forests are poor and burdened with debt to the developed world. Our own major High Street banks are beneficiaries of their repayments and the interest that they pay on their loans, as well as our government, and of course the World Bank and the International Monetary Fund. How are these countries going to find cash for these repayments? Logging is part of the answer.

Yet despite all this, the reasons for stopping the erosion of the world's tropical forests are compelling. It would not matter so much if it was happening on a small scale, but the rate of erosion is enormous. Some 17 million hectares of tropical forests are lost each year. The best estimate is that just 1.5 billion hectares of undisturbed primary forest still remain out of the 6.2 billion that existed before settled agriculture began. No secondary forest or plantation can begin to compete with the biological richness or ecological importance of primary forest. It has been well said that 'while debate rages over how much ancient forest to protect, the last stands are disappearing'. Moreover, the demand for wood is at an all-time high and continues to grow, while poor countries badly need cash for development. This is a calamitous situation which will threaten the natural support systems of so many people. If anyone were to ask me what is the chief curse of modern technology, I would reply straightaway: the chainsaw. How can it be restrained? What can governments do about it? What can we do about it?

In the first place, we need to reduce the demand for wood generally. Until an acceptable substitute is found for wood used for pulping into paper, we can at least insist on recycled paper. This means that we not only buy recycled paper, but we also keep our waste paper for recycling; and this is not easily achieved in some areas. There could be saving too in the way paper is used. If all photocopying were done on both sides of the paper, thousands of tons would be saved! There is also much industrial waste of wood, both in the building trade and in manufacture. Human nature being what it is, probably only increases in price will achieve these economies.

Countries are sovereign states and they can do what they like with their own resources. I suspect that the Third World countries will only stop cutting down the ancient tropical rain forests when they realize that it is in their own longer-term interest to do so. It has been estimated that 1 hectare of Peruvian rain forest could provide six times more revenue in non-timber products than could be made through the sale of timber. When people begin to realize that logging will wreck their future economy, and that it is essential to set up a system of sustainable forestry management, then the situation will change. But for this to happen they will need help and encouragement from wealthier countries, especially those which at present buy their timber products. One of the more promising ideas is the 'debt for conservation' scheme, whereby countries agree to conserve forests in return for being let off some of the huge repayments and interest on their debts.

The environmental pressure groups are generally opposed to the policies of both the European Community and of our government over the tropical rain forests. This is not the place to enter into the complex details of international organizations which have been set up for logging projects and for reafforestation. While the official policy is to rely on these schemes for the future, the voluntary agencies complain of their inefficiency and say that they are not in fact stopping the forests from being cut down.

* * *

What I'm saying may seem remote to people sitting in a pew. But do not forget that your pew is made of wood, and that is what this sermon is all about – wood. And there are practical suggestions which can be made. You can economize on paper, you can buy recycled paper, and you can give your waste paper for recycling. When buying new furniture, or doors or window frames, you can make certain that you are not buying wood from the tropical rain forests. And there is another suggestion that I would like to make to you which I hope you will find rewarding. Think about the blessings God gives us through trees: the shade, the shelter, the leaves, the beauty. Think of their height, their strength, such that it takes a hurricane to blow them

26

down. Think of the cedars of Lebanon, so admired in Old Testament times. I might just as well have taken my text from Ezekiel, who mentions trees so often in his prophecies. Jesus himself borrowed one of these when he spoke about a grain of mustard seed which grew bigger than all the trees, so that all the birds nestled under its branches. He says the Kingdom of God is like a tree. We must not, we cannot, be indifferent to trees.

6

OZONE

*And the fourth angel poured out his vial upon the sun; and power
was given unto him to scorch men with fire. And men were
scorched with great heat, and blasphemed the name of God, which
hath power over these plagues: and they repented not to give him
glory.*

REVELATION 16.8–9 (AV)

How often have you been badly sunburnt in Britain? We who live in a
temperate zone are not always aware of the sun's strength, if only
because we so seldom feel it. It quite takes us by surprise on the few
occasions when it is hot enough to do us harm. Do you holiday
abroad? If so, you will know far better the heat and power of the sun's
rays. People who lie on their backs, almost sizzling with heat, by the
blue Mediterranean sea or by the hotel swimming pool, have to take
precautions against sunburn by applying layers of what are nowadays
somewhat quaintly called 'sun blockers'. Even the fact that it is now
possible (according to the advertisements) to develop a deep natural
tan without the aid of the sun does not deter people from invading the
Mediterranean regions and tropical resorts so that they can return
home tanned and brown.

DEPLETION OF THE OZONE LAYER, ITS CAUSES AND EFFECTS

The sun is the source of all our energy, and without its life-giving
warmth we could not live. Nonetheless, the rays of the sun can have
harmful effects other than sunburn. In particular, the sun emits
dangerous very short-wave ultraviolet rays, but fortunately over 95
per cent of these are absorbed by a layer of ozone which lies in the
stratosphere which stretches 10–50 miles above the earth. (Ozone is a
gas made up of molecules of three oxygen atoms. It is dangerous for us
at ground level, but it performs this vital protective function for us in
the stratosphere.) In 1974 it was discovered that certain gases could

28

cause this ozone layer to be depleted. Some feared that the supersonic Concorde, flying so high above the earth, would emit gases which would do just that, although it became clear that such a small fleet of these aircraft would only have a negligible effect. (When Concorde Mark II is built, it may be a different story if large numbers come into service.) In 1984 it was discovered that there was an actual hole in the ozone layer around the South Pole. Later another hole was discovered around the North Pole, and elsewhere the layer has been found to have diminished in size: in the Northern hemisphere by up to 3 per cent within little more than a decade. And by 1990 it was discovered that the gaps at the poles had widened.

What is the effect of ozone depletion? The very short waves of ultraviolet (known as UVB) can cause cancer. It is believed that a 1 per cent decrease in ozone levels results in a 3 per cent increase in certain skin cancers. Among these is malignant melanoma: nearly half of those who contract this die within five years, and people with fair skins are particularly affected. UVB can also cause eye disease, and affect the immunosuppressive systems of the human body, the same effect as that of the HIV virus which causes AIDS.

There are, however, equally serious effects on agriculture and the marine environment. The United States Environmental Protection Agency has discovered that nearly two-thirds of the plant species that it has investigated, such as peas, beans, and varieties of wheat and soya bean, are sensitive to UVB radiation, resulting in reduced agricultural yields worldwide. What is more, the tiny marine organisms such as zooplankton or phytoplankton in the oceans would be damaged. These micro-organisms play a crucial part in the planet's ecosystems. They also affect the food chains. Since the bigger animals eat smaller ones, marine life would be affected all the way from shrimps to seals, whales and seabirds. Not a welcome prospect!

What had caused this ozone depletion? The story about how this problem was discovered is a fascinating one, including balloons, aeroplanes and a home-made gadget constructed by a scientist friend of mine which can measure gas as thin as one part in a trillion. But such a story is hardly suited to a sermon! It is now established that five gases contribute to the ozone depletion. These gases do not easily disperse, and in time ascend into the stratosphere. Some of them have long and difficult names and for this reason they are known by their initials. (In fact, you don't seem to progress very far in the world these days without acronyms, initials which stand for titles.)

The first of these gases are the chlorofluorocarbons, better known as CFCs. These are used for the cooling apparatus in fridges, as insulation for buildings, and as cleaners for electrical components. The food industry depends a great deal on refrigeration, which prevents food deteriorating. If we have fridges in our own houses, we are hardly in a position to deny them to those who haven't. Fortunately, their use in fridges is already being phased out. The other day I incautiously hastened on the defrosting process in our fridge at home and punctured the deep freezer compartment. A hiss and a cloud of gas resulted. After hastily ringing up the manufacturer, I was relieved to find out that I had not released CFCs which would ascend in due time to the stratosphere!

The second set of gases, less ozone depleting, are the hydrochlorofluorocarbons, known as HCFCs. These are also used in fridges, but also as foam, as solvents and in aerosols. Once again, substitutes are needed as soon as possible. But care has to be taken with the properties of replacement material. A famous British firm, for example, produced a replacement for CFCs which was nearly 6,000 times as effective as a global warming gas as carbon dioxide!

The third gas is methyl chloroform, used for metal cleaning, in the manufacture of some adhesives, and in electronic cleaning. These are important uses, and once again some acceptable alternative must be found.

The same holds good for carbon tetrachloride, used in many chemical processes. Other particularly important gases are the halons, used in fire extinguishers, which are very necessary for civilized living! And so these gases that are having such a terrible effect on the ozone layer are extremely useful. Naturally, manufacturers count the cost of new plant and new technologies. But the laws of countries have to be changed, forbidding their use. They must be phased out. We cannot permit such danger to human beings, danger to plants, and danger to marine life. We seem to be removing the very safeguards to life which God in his providence has given us.

THE MEANING OF THE TEXT

And here I turn at last to my text – about time too, you may think – because this is a sermon about the word of God, not a lecture about obscure chemical processes. My text, you may remember, came from the Book of Revelation. It was about one of the plagues which, it prophesied, God in his anger would inflict on the children of men: the plague of the sun which scorched humans with fire. The account of these plagues is very striking; and although the fourth plague which I took as my text bears some resemblance to the perils from the 'ozone gap', it would be quite wrong to regard this as the fulfilment of prophecy from the Book of Revelation. In the first place, the plague in the Scripture is the result of God's wrath, whereas our present danger lies rather in what we have been doing in ignorance to our environment – unless we take the wrath of God to mean, as Professor Dodd used to interpret it, the transgression of the natural law. The ozone layer was essential if human life was to develop on earth, and with the eye of faith we can look on it as part of God's providential care for the life that he has created; yet we are destroying it. In any case, we are hardly *scorched* by ultraviolet rays.

Secondly, people are not blaspheming the name of the Lord because of what is happening to our environment; indeed, those who call on the name of the Lord and those who don't are equally to blame. Nor can it be said that Christians have played a particularly notable role in the international negotiations that have been taking place to enable the planet to be blanketed with an ozone layer as it used to be. That has been done by environmentalists and by supporters of 'green movements'. Nor, in the third place, can it be alleged that such people have not 'repented to give God the glory'. On the contrary, they have treated the matter as entirely secular.

But of course it's not just that. The way in which we treat our environment, whether on the earth or in the oceans or in the air, betrays our inner attitudes towards the natural world which God has given us to enjoy. It is our duty to ensure that others – whether they belong to other parts of the world or to future generations – can enjoy it too, and that we do not cause unnecessary harm to other species of God's creation. This duty which we owe to our brothers and sisters, and to other orders of life besides our own, is part of the duty which we owe to God the Creator of all. Certainly it is to our self-interest to restore the ozone layer as promptly as possible, but then, as Archbishop William Temple said, the art of government is the art of so ordering life that self-interest prompts what justice demands. And justice to our fellow men and women and to future generations does demand that we rectify the ozone gap.

ENCOURAGING DEVELOPMENTS

Here a wonderful beginning has already been made. Our environmental problems are such that to recount them often seems like an unmitigated account of gloom and doom. Not so with ozone. For the first time in history, the nations of the world have agreed to work together

31

to save our environment. In the Montreal Convention they agreed to reduce the production of ozone-reducing gases. Even more important, in 1989 no less than 81 governments signed a declaration agreeing to phase out the production and use of CFCs by the year 2000; to phase out halons 'as soon as feasible'; to restrict other ozone-reducing substances; and to tighten up the timetable – at the same time giving due regard to the position of developing countries.

The Third World did not produce the problem but the First World did. So the developed countries have agreed to transfer their technologies to the Third World, and to assist in financing change, while the countries which used the smallest amount of these substances were allowed further time to make the required changes. This is enormously encouraging and gives hope for the future. The nations of the world can co-operate when it is in the interest of all to ensure that this happens. However, the ozone gap will not disappear overnight. Far from it. Interim cuts are important in moving towards a complete phase-out. If 50 per cent cuts could be made by 1995, the ozone hole would be eliminated ten years sooner. On the other hand, each five-year delay in the phase-out of these ozone-depleting gases delays the time needed to eliminate the Antarctic hole by eighteen years. Chlorine levels, due to CFCs, are already 500 times more than normal and, even if we phased out all these gases by 1995, chlorine levels would not return to normal until the twenty-second century. It will be a long haul, but we will get there in the end; or rather, our great-great-great-great-great-great-great-great-grandchildren will get there!

*　*　*

Meanwhile, *we* still live in the twentieth century. What can we do? Quite a lot! When replacing an old fridge, we can check that if it contains CFCs they will be safely disposed of. If we buy a new fridge, we can find one without CFCs. We can look for 'ozone friendly' labels, especially on aerosols. And if you can afford to buy a car with air conditioning, don't. It's unnecessary in Britain, and there is no CFC-free alternative.

We should thank God for the natural protection that he gives us in so many ways, especially through the ozone layer. He puts a hedge about us so often which we take for granted; and then in our folly and ignorance we tend to knock it down. He gives us knowledge through science and technology to change our environment.

We must insist that it is used not to harm the world, but to embellish it.

7

NUCLEAR POWER

The day of the Lord will come as a thief in the night; in which
the heavens shall pass away with a great noise, and the elements
shall melt with fervent heat, the earth also and the works that
are therein shall be burned up.

2 PETER 3.10 (AV)

EXPLANATION OF THE TEXT

My text comes from the so-called second epistle of St Peter, generally
agreed to be the last book of the New Testament to be written, and
very improbably coming from the hand of Peter the apostle – although
the person who wrote it believed in good faith that he was standing in
the tradition of the Great Fisherman. One of the reasons why it does
not appear to be from the hand of the apostle is that part of it seems to
be taken from the epistle of St Jude. The author, whoever he was,
introduces this fiery end to the universe in order to encourage his
readers to be, in his own words, 'of holy conversation and godliness'.
He thought that the end of all things was at hand, in common with the
Jewish Christian tradition of his day. In the light of our scientific
knowledge, we think otherwise today, although of course we never
know when a comet or meteorite might strike the earth. Only a year or
two ago, the question arose whether there should be a warning about
one such 'planetesimal', although fortunately for us the wandering
heavenly body missed us by a large margin. But this was not the case
with the meteorite or meteorites that probably brought to an end the
age of the dinosaurs. (Incidentally, it was providential for us that this
happened, because otherwise we could scarcely have evolved from the
small species of mammal that survived, which was only the size of a
rat!)

In fact, the author of 2 Peter wrote more truly than he realized. The
sun will gradually use up its hydrogen as it converts it into helium
and, as it does this, it will grow in luminosity – it has already increased
by some 30 per cent since life appeared on earth. This will go on until
the oceans boil! The sun will swell up into what is known among

astronomers as a 'red giant' and actually engulf the earth. Life of course would have long become extinct. But that is a comfortable span away from us today – there are some ten billion years to go!

NUCLEAR BOMBS

The author of 2 Peter speaks of this event as 'the day of the Lord'. This phrase could be used not only of the end of all things, but also of some current catastrophe. For example, in the gospels the fall of Jerusalem is described in this way. And the explosion of a nuclear weapon might also merit that description, especially modern hydrogen bombs which are so much more powerful than the one dropped by the Allies on Hiroshima. If that be the case, then the description in 2 Peter appears to be remarkably accurate. For when a bomb explodes there is a terrible noise, and the heat is so intense that the elements do melt, and the earth and all that is built on it are burnt up. I happened to be lecturing in Japan a year or two ago, and I joined in a meal with the Anglican parish of Hiroshima. There were thirteen people there who had been in Hiroshima when the bomb was dropped: fortunately, they lived in the suburbs. The city is now totally rebuilt, but the area where the bomb fell has been kept bare as a memorial, and only one building is standing. The museum is horrifying; but I found to my surprise some Japanese Christians who approved of it having been dropped, because it ended what would have been a protracted and bloody war.

I mention nuclear weapons, because it was on this account that nuclear power was first developed, and there was a race between Germany and the Allies to see who could get it first. Now we have it, the secret of how to produce a nuclear bomb is out, and we have to live with this knowledge. When I was Dean of a Cambridge college, the Master of my college had been in charge of the British team in the USA which helped to produce the bomb; and he was so appalled at its effects that he never again entered a laboratory after the war ended. Christians are of course divided over whether it is right or wrong for one nation to use force against another, and again they are divided about whether it can be right to keep nuclear weapons as a deterrent, and even whether it could ever be right to use them. Although tension has been relaxed by the signing of the START Treaty by the USA and the USSR in 1991, this only reduces nuclear long-range missiles to 7,000 on each side, the number that existed when these talks first began; and recent events in the former USSR have made people nervous about the custody of their nuclear weapons. Christians ought to go on thinking about these matters, but I am not going to enter into that debate today.

But it needs to be said that one of the main reasons why people are so frightened of nuclear power is that nuclear bombs can easily be made by those who have the necessary nuclear ingredients. There is a non-proliferation treaty, but people like Saddam Hussein take no notice of that. There was even a handbook printed in the USA showing how an individual could put together a DIY nuclear weapon in his backyard. He needs a little plutonium, but it is very difficult for nuclear establishments to keep track of all the plutonium that they handle, and there is always the chance that determined raiders might be able to invade a nuclear plant and steal some. But I think that we have to admit that we cannot put the clock back. People now know the science underlying nuclear weapons, and the technology needed to construct them. That knowledge cannot be unlearnt.

NUCLEAR RISKS

There are of course other dangers which we associate with nuclear power apart from nuclear war. Accidents happen, whether at a nuclear plant or in transporting irradiated material. Extraordinary mistakes can be made. In Illinois, after a cooling problem, a complete welding machine was found to have been left in the reactor vessel. Fortunately there was no accident.

Accidents can have terrible effects. In this country we were lucky that our accident at Windscale happened as early as in 1957, forcing us to tighten our safety margins. But its memory is so painful that the place name has had to be changed to Sellafield. The worst case would be a core meltdown with a consequent explosion akin to a nuclear bomb. This nearly happened at Three Mile Island in the USA and half happened at Chernobyl in the USSR. People are still suffering as a result. There is a reactor in Bulgaria at Kosloduy which supplies 40 per cent of its energy. It is said to be in a very dangerous state. If it were closed down, though, Bulgaria would have insufficient energy for its industries. Apart from this large-scale danger, there is also a risk for those who work in nuclear establishments, and for those who live nearby. For example, there is a higher incidence of leukaemia among children in the vicinity of Sellafield (though no conclusive evidence that this is caused by nuclear radiation).

At the same time, we have to face the fact that life is full of risks.

The question to be asked is not whether the production of energy by nuclear fission is dangerous, but whether the risks are such that it is wrong to use this means of production. Major accidents will always occur in any industry. At the moment, accidents from nuclear power are far less frequent than those incurred by mining coal or by the use of the car! This fact is too easily forgotten, because people are frightened of the unknown, and nuclear radiation is invisible. Nuclear energy is easily monitored and figures sound rather terrifying when we do not know what they really mean. Most people in places like Aberdeen, the granite city, who may be frightened of nuclear energy, are blissfully unaware of the nuclear radiation which is emitted from their granite houses.

There is however one form of risk of which we should be particularly aware, and that is the risk that we pass on to future generations. Originally the British nuclear programme was meant to lead up to the installation of 'fast breeder reactors' – so called because they bred more plutonium than they used in creating energy. At one time, the threat of breeder reactors was so great that with the encouragement of Mr Wedgwood Benn, the Energy Minister, I organized a series of public hearings on the subject on behalf of the British Council of Churches. However, the threat has receded, because of the failure of the British research programme based on Dounreay to come up with a safe and economic system for commercial production.

The type of nuclear reactor which is in use today produces nuclear wastes and material for nuclear reprocessing. Risks are involved with both of these, but particularly for future generations in the permanent disposal of material with high levels of nuclear radiation. For the time being, these have been stored in steel containers in Sellafield. Where and how are they to be permanently stored? A process of reducing them to solid glass substances is said to be perfectly safe, but of course no one can tell what will happen to them over a period of 10,000 years! It seems unfair to land posterity with this as well as with the problem of rendering safe a nuclear installation when it has ended its useful life. The public needs reassurance (which may well be given) that the risks of danger to posterity are not great.

There are those who think that to produce nuclear energy is to take on the role of God. It is an interference with the natural order of things on earth which, they say, is bound to rebound upon us. A little reflection, however, will show that this is a false kind of argument. In fact, the energy in the universe comes from nuclear energy produced in the interior of its stars. That is why they burn bright. When God created his universe, he intended it to be powered by nuclear energy.

And so why should not his creatures use the same kind of energy on earth?

There are economic reasons for the decline of nuclear power. The high hopes originally entertained about it have not been fulfilled. Our original nuclear reactors have done sterling service, but they now are reaching the end of their natural lives. Since then our nuclear programme has run into the sand. There has been great disappointment over the construction of nuclear plant. First, we built the wrong kind of reactor, and then, when we changed over to gas-cooled reactors, there were enormous cost overruns, so that nuclear power is more expensive to produce than energy from fossil fuels. There will be further huge expenses in decommissioning worn-out reactors. The nuclear programme is only kept in being on political grounds so as provide an alternative means of energy: these do not concern us here.

I know that many will disagree with me, but I can't see any inordinate risk in our present nuclear programmes. If, however, every country were to get the whole of its energy from nuclear fission, the risks would then be too great. One day perhaps nuclear energy may become available not from nuclear fission but from nuclear fusion, although there is no prospect of this at present. If safe, cheap and superabundant energy from this other source of nuclear energy were ever to become available, I doubt whether humanity would be able to exercise sufficient self-restraint in its use to conserve the ecosystems of the planet.

★ ★ ★

Is there any message here from the Lord for you and me? We are bound to live with risk in one form or another. Naturally we seek to minimize that risk, whether it be risk from nuclear power or from insufficient energy for our needs. Risk is unavoidable in living as human beings. What we all need is sufficient grace to cope with the hazards of life, so that we are neither unduly fearful, nor take undue risks. Grace is the gift of God, and we need to pray for grace for ourselves and for others.

8

GLOBAL WARMING

*In them hath he set a tabernacle for the sun, which cometh forth as
a bridegroom out of his chamber, and rejoiceth as a giant to run
his course. It goeth forth from the uttermost part of the heaven and
runneth about unto the end of it again; and there is nothing hid
from the heat thereof.*

PSALM 19.5–6

Light, heat, energy – they all come from the sun! No wonder that we
call people who bask in the sun 'sun worshippers'. In fact, there are
religions in which people do actually worship the sun. The Psalmist
knew better: the sun is part of God's creation. He thought of it as a
giant who came out of his tent with all the energy of a newly married
man, and did his daily jog from one end of the heavens to another.
Today we know that we move round the sun rather than the sun
round us, and that the turning of the earth around its own axis divides
the day from the night, depending on which way we face. The sun is
one of God's good gifts to all his creatures, and given, like the rain, to
the just and the unjust alike. No wonder St Francis thanked God for
'our brother the Sun'.

THE GREENHOUSE EFFECT

It is literally true that all the energy we use on this planet (other than
that which comes from nuclear power) comes directly or indirectly
from the sun. The same is not quite true of the earth, because its core
is molten; but without the sun the air would be unimaginably cold and
no life would be remotely possible. In places like England we could do
with more direct sunshine, and we would like the temperature to be
higher than it is. In fact, quite a few people extend their houses to
make a conservatory. The very word indicates that heat is conserved.
This is because the warmth of the sun comes through the glass in the
conservatory, but it cannot all get out again, and so it is conserved.
This is the 'greenhouse effect' and, thank goodness, it takes place

naturally in our atmosphere. Without the gases which act like a conservatory, our temperature would be some 30 degrees Centigrade lower than it is. It is in fact part of God's marvellous providence that our temperature remains stable, and has done so over millions of years since life began – despite the fact that the sun has increased in luminosity by nearly a third!

Unfortunately we have been tampering unwittingly with this wonderful balance of nature. We have been producing more greenhouse gases than can be absorbed by natural processes. The result, as scientists agree, is that the planet is either already beginning to warm up, or is almost certain to do so very soon. (The unfortunate eruption of Mt Pinatubo is likely to delay global warming because all the dust particles circulating in the upper atmosphere will impede the sun's rays. Because of this, some people will say that the threat of warming is only a scare, but there is general agreement among most scientists that it is real.) By the year 2025 it would be on average 1 degree Centigrade warmer, and by the end of the century 3 degrees warmer – and that is hotter than it has been for the last 2 million years! You may think that this is not much, but if we do not take steps worldwide to stop this process we shall find devastating effects ensue. There would be some melting of ice at the poles, and so the height of the sea would rise, which would be devastating for low-lying countries like the Low Countries or Bangladesh. If nothing is done, the oceans would rise 2½ inches every ten years, and in just over a century this would affect nearly a quarter of a million miles of the world's coastlines (including that of Britain). There would also be changes in the climate and in the weather. Granted, this has happened before. But this time it would happen too quickly for natural vegetation and crops to adapt to it. Some land would become infertile. It is possible that the greater warmth could spark off new viruses and illnesses, and extend the scope of tropical diseases. Agriculture and natural ecosystems would be damaged. It is not difficult to imagine the effect this would have in a world where population is increasing and food production cannot keep up. And what is more, there is some danger of a runaway effect. The stability of our climate is a wonderful natural example of divine providence which we simply take for granted; and the systems that ensure it have great elasticity. But elastic that is overstretched can break. It is not impossible that one effect could give rise to another. For example, if ice and snow melted at the poles, there would be less albedo or whiteness to reflect heat back into space, and this would add further to the greenhouse effect. The increasing heat would enable methane gas to escape from the frozen tundra.

It would be wrong to inflict all these terrible effects on posterity.

39

We must be better stewards of our planet. God owns its freehold, not us: we only have a repairing lease, and we had better look to our repairs.

GASES THAT CAUSE THE GREENHOUSE EFFECT

What are the gases that contribute to the greenhouse effect, and how can we reverse what they are doing? One group that has brought about the ozone gap is CFCs and HCFCs (chlorofluorocarbons and hydrochlorofluorocarbons), and this group accounts for a quarter of the trouble with the greenhouse effect too. When released, these gases make their way up into the stratosphere where they diminish the ozone layer which is essential for health. It is agreed that the use of these gases must be phased out, as we have already seen when thinking about the ozone layer. Ozone itself at ground level is a greenhouse gas, making up about 12 per cent of the total of greenhouse gases. It is formed by sunlight acting on pollutants from factories, cars and other sources. Another such gas is nitrous oxide, but this is given off by vegetation and soils, and there is nothing we can do about it.

Another gas is methane, and this is responsible for about 15 per cent of the trouble. It is a particularly bad 'greenhouse gas' compared with the others. One of the ways that this gas is produced is by substances decaying when the air can't get at them. It has a nasty smell. We find it in marshlands and wetlands, and also in organic rubbish when buried. In the West Midlands, Lord Aylesford, the Lord Lieutenant, built up on his estate enormous tips from the rubbish of the neighbouring conurbation, large enough to be landscaped into hillocks. He actually put pipes in for methane gas and sold it locally! Within two or three years, 70 such schemes are expected to be in operation. Another source of methane is from the digestive tracts of livestock, from their belches and flatulence, and to a lesser extent from their excrement when it is not open to the air. Livestock account for 3 per cent of all greenhouse gases. There are other reasons why we urgently need to breed fewer livestock, and this would lessen their contribution to the greenhouse effect.

By far the largest contribution to global warming, indeed some half of the total, is made by carbon dioxide – so large a contribution that I must spend the rest of this sermon talking about it. Carbon dioxide is released by you, me and every other living thing when we breathe, die and decay. But we are not contributing to the greenhouse effect by every breath that we exhale, because by a wonderful provision of

40

divine providence our carbon dioxide is taken up by plants and trees which break it up, taking up the carbon, and releasing oxygen which purifies the atmosphere. But when organic material is burnt, especially timber, this releases carbon dioxide back into the atmosphere. And so the burning of stubble and heathland and the clearing of forests for agriculture all contribute to the greenhouse effect. This is happening on a massive scale, mostly in the Third World. There are other reasons why the felling of forests must be reduced as well as the carbon dioxide which results from burning them. I have preached a sermon on trees and forests on an earlier occasion, and so I will not repeat the details now.

It is the burning of the so-called fossil fuels which is far and away the worst offender in the production of carbon dioxide (called CO_2 because it consists of one atom of carbon and two atoms of oxygen). The initiative for the reduction of carbon dioxide must come from the industrialized world. Although it comprises less than a quarter of the world's population, it is responsible for 90 per cent of greenhouse gases and, so far as CO_2 is concerned, for 70 per cent of the fossil fuels that are burnt (if we do not count the burning oil wells in Kuwait for most of 1991). If you are an average Briton, you are responsible for the burning of 10.8 tonnes of fossil fuel each year. If you are an average American, you are responsible for 18.5 tonnes; but if you are from a poor African country, only for 0.15 tonnes a year. Britain is the sixth worst in the carbon dioxide league, with the USA by far the worst of all.

FOSSIL FUELS

You may well ask, what do we use these fossil fuels for? I won't bother you here with precise percentages. Let me just tell you that nearly a quarter goes on refining petrol and driving motor vehicles on the roads, 20 per cent is used in our homes, nearly a quarter goes on industry which makes the things we buy, and over a third on power stations which make our electricity – most of which is produced by coal (although the new power companies propose to use more gas, which is less polluting, and are being forced to obtain some of their energy from alternative sources). How then can we go on producing more and more things, and at the same time cut down on the carbon dioxide that we produce? It will involve a massive effort by every one of us, and even then there is bound to be a limit to production. Even farmers will have to do something too, because vast amounts of fossil

41

fuel are used in manufacturing pesticides and artificial fertilizers. You might remember that the next time you visit your garden centre!

In the first place we waste an enormous amount of our fossil fuels. Let me come down to earth and be very practical. Did you realize that more gas is lost in cracked pipes than burnt? I wonder how well insulated your house is? I wonder whether you only fill the kettle as full as you need? Do you always use your washing machine with a full load? When you buy an electrical appliance, do you ask how 'energy efficient' it is? Do you buy 'long-life' light bulbs? This list of questions is getting embarrassing, and it could go on and on. If we are inefficient in our use of energy at home, think of the way offices are overheated, think how industry could be more economic about its energy. Did you know that even in our temperate climate, an office building can be constructed which is entirely heated by people's body warmth?

AN EXCITING NEW DEVELOPMENT

An exciting new technique for the treatment of coal has been developed, and it is surprising that it is not yet generally known. I suppose it has been kept secret for financial reasons. The research department of one of the major oil companies has devised a method of carbon dioxide recovery, so that coal may be burnt without any harmful emissions. The coal is converted to hydrogen and CO_2 with no gaseous effluent, and then the hydrogen may be burnt in a fuel cell just as efficiently as coal is burnt in a current generating plant. If this were done at our electricity-generating stations, it would mean that there would be no need of filters because there would be no harmful emissions which cause acid rain. More importantly, such a method of using coal would not contribute in any way to the greenhouse effect. Admittedly, with the fuel cell, it would be 30 per cent more expensive, but, if the costs of reducing pollution from conventional burning are taken into account, the difference is comparatively slight. This development shows both the advantages and the limitations of the 'technological fix'. On the one hand, it would enable the burning of a fossil fuel without any of the present disadvantages; and that is a great gain. On the other hand, it could only be used in large plants where a great deal of coal is burnt (such as generating stations) and it would not have any impact on the burning of gas or oil, except in so far as coal is substituted for them – and the scope for substitution would be very limited. And it would not be the long-term answer to the problem of energy use, because reserves of coal are limited. We would also need alternative sources of energy.

ALTERNATIVE SOURCES OF ENERGY

Alternatives to fossil fuels are needed. We can put aside nuclear power; we looked at that earlier. We decided that we cannot risk world-scale production of energy from that source. There is not much chance of making use of the heat from the earth's molten core; and burning rubbish will not produce much energy, and is likely to produce some carbon dioxide even if burnt at a high temperature. For cars there is as yet no alternative to fossil fuels. But for other uses, let us remember the sun 'which cometh forth as a bridegroom out of his chamber, and rejoiceth as a giant to run his course'. The energy of the sun can either be used through solar panels for helping to heat water, or for the direct production of electricity through photovoltaic cells. Already we can power a pocket calculator through a photoelectric cell; but unfortunately, direct energy production from a solar cell is not yet economically viable on a commercial scale. But big advances are being made, and we are getting nearer the time when, with mass production, this will be possible. Indirect forms of solar heating include tidal barrages (the tides are the result of gravity at work within the solar system), wind power (because it is the heat of the sun that causes the wind) and wave power (because the waves are stirred up by the wind). Research in Britain on these has been centred on Harwell, which is the nuclear research centre. Some of us think that this has resulted in their not being given a fair share of our research money, and there has been some evidence of fudging over the costs of wave power. Whether or not this is so, Britain used to be in the vanguard of research, but has now slipped right back. At long last wave power is beginning to be used (and we have a long shoreline) and wind power too (and there is plenty of wind!). A fillip has been given by the requirement that the privatized power companies must produce some energy from alternative sources. But British plans are minute compared, say, with those of Denmark, and even British government advisers report that, if the will were there, half of British electricity could come from these sources within twenty years! Here lies the future of energy resources, especially as fossil fuel reserves run out.

The British government has pledged that by the year 2005 carbon dioxide emissions will be cut back to the levels of 1990. Without restraint it is reckoned they would have increased by 30 per cent by

43

the year 2005 – not very far off. I wish there were more signs of urgency. But if sacrifices must be made, they must be agreed all round; this points to the great importance of the United Nations Conference on the Environment in Brazil in 1992.

May I ask you to pray for all people and countries involved in that conference, and for a will to carry out whatever is agreed, to make the world safer for posterity? Even if they do not agree, *we must not give up*. Change is always possible.

9
MOTOR CARS

And the watchman told, saying . . . the driving is like the driving
of Jehu the son of Nimshi; for he driveth furiously.
2 KINGS 9.20 (AV)

DRIVING FAST

It's hardly surprising that Jehu was driving furiously, because at the
time he was engaged in a typical colonels' plot in the Middle East of
the kind which still occurs today; and no doubt at such a moment
speed was of the essence. In any case, he would hardly have been
going at more than 30 mph, for he only had a crude two-horsepower
vehicle (or was it four-horsepower?) as he drove his chariot towards
the king of Israel. Nowadays we have far more powerful and speedy
vehicles powered by the internal combustion engine and fuelled by
petrol, and we no longer assess their strength in terms of horsepower
but by the size of the engine – 1,500 cc or whatever. The faster we
drive the more vehicles guzzle up precious fossil fuels, although we
don't often think of that. We drive our cars furiously not for reasons
of state like Jehu, but because we like to indulge ourselves. We like
driving fast. It is exhilarating and it gives us a sense of power and
virility; and in any case, life in the modern world seems a constant
rush. We are not always as polite on the road as we could be, because
the windscreen somehow seems to divorce us from reality. The faster
we drive, the more pollution our cars emit, and the more likely there
is to be an accident. Apart from 300,000 people injured on British
roads, 4,500 people are killed by motor vehicles every year; but,
although that is 4,500 too many, at least the death rate on British
roads is low compared with other countries.

THE NEED FOR RESTRAINT IN THE USE OF CARS

At whatever speed we drive it, the motor car is a wonderful invention
for transporting people. I am sure everyone here who owns a car

would agree with that. It gives us personalized travel in our own time when we want it. We move from A to B without even getting out of our seat! Compared with public transport, it seems cheap (although in fact there are hidden costs). Above all, it is a boon for those of us with children. We throw all their paraphernalia into the boot, and make off carefree on our journey. We can drive them to school. At a pinch, we can even sleep in the car – or, if we prefer a caravan, we can tow it behind us. With modern styling the car is often an object of beauty, and frequently treated as such. Some people wash their car more frequently than they wash their hair. I don't decry the motor car, because I possess one myself. I don't know what I would do without it, for I am often invited to preach on a Sunday morning and I have to set out before public transport is functioning properly.

If one speaks out against the use of the motor car, one is often understood to be totally against it. This was why, on my nomination as Bishop of Birmingham, the motor car city, the local newspaper ran a campaign against me for a whole month! In fact, I think that it would be unfair to try to prevent anyone who wants a car from buying one. That would be élitist in attitude. It's bad enough, in a country like Britain where public transport has been so neglected in the past, that only one person in three owns a car, and as a result many are at a disadvantage; and although two out of three families have a car, often it is not available on weekdays because one of the family uses it to go to work. We need restrictions not on the sale of motor cars, but on their use.

There are two reasons for this. The first one is that if there are too many cars on the roads, the roads become jammed. The problem is not solved simply by building more roads, because this simply results in more cars to jam them up. By trying to suit our own convenience, we only add to the inconvenience of others besides ourselves. There are even stronger moral reasons for the restriction of motor-car use, and these are because of the effect on the environment.

LEVELS OF CONCERN

There are three distinct levels of environmental concern. The first affects you and me directly. We do not like to see motorways gouging their way through beautiful unspoilt countryside. We do not like what the experts call 'visual intrusion'. We do not like great chunks of our lovely countryside covered with concrete and tarmac. Even though we now have to have some agricultural land taken out of use as 'set aside', we do not like to see other good land eaten up by making provision for the motor car. The first level of environmental concern affects our own personal interests.

The second level of concern over cars affects you and me on a national scale. It was worse when everyone used leaded petrol. Lead is toxic, and there is good scientific evidence that even small quantities of lead ingested by small children retard their intellectual development. I was engaged in the campaign to get the petrol companies to produce the unleaded variety. I used to watch children playing in the road near Spaghetti Junction in Birmingham, and I knew that when they sucked their thumbs they would be ingesting lead from the dust in the street. In the end the government was won over, but it was a difficult battle. Fortunately, unleaded petrol is now available at a discount price and many use it. The campaign to bring this about was financed personally out of the pocket of a wealthy and generous Jewish businessman. He cares about the environment. I found it rather shaming that wealthy and generous Christian businessmen did not seem to care as much.

ENVIRONMENTAL POLLUTION

Cars and lorries emit noxious fumes. If you have ever driven behind a car which needs decarbonizing, you will know that filthy cloud of smoke belching out of its exhaust. (This is actually against the law, but the police have more urgent matters to attend to.) There are also other pollutants which you cannot see. One of these is the very poisonous carbon monoxide. A common way of committing suicide is to fix up a hosepipe from the exhaust into the main body of a car, shut the windows and switch on the ignition; tragically, the occupant of the car goes to sleep and does not wake up. Fortunately, in the open air this gas is no problem. But in hot weather, when there is no wind, nitrogen oxides among the exhaust gases interact with the sunlight and form ozone. The exhaust gases can also create that brown haze we call photochemical smog. If you have a tendency to asthma, it will not help you! Researchers reckon it kills 30,000 a year in the USA. The pollution can be so bad that people are told not to leave their houses. These nitrogen oxides also cause acid rain, about which I am preaching separately. Exhaust gases also contribute to global warming. You may be wanting to reply to me that these noxious exhaust fumes will be vastly reduced by the introduction of catalytic converters fixed to the exhaust, some of which are already in use. Unfortunately, the

47

estimated increase in car usage will overwhelm the reduction in the emission of these gases from individual cars. The Department of Transport estimates a maximum increase of 140 per cent in British car ownership in the next fifty years!

GLOBAL CONCERN

I said that there were three levels of environmental concern, and the third affects you and me on a global scale. This brings me to the one form of pollution that no filter can reduce. When we burn fossil fuels we produce carbon dioxide. Petrol is a liquid refined from deposits which have been laid down in the earth from prehistoric forests. When these carbon-based fuels are burnt they produce carbon dioxide; and this is a global warming gas. Some 17 per cent of all carbon dioxide released into the atmosphere comes from burning fossil fuels. Your car and mine, without doubt, are helping to warm up the atmosphere of the globe. Admittedly, your car is only one among 400 million; but the worldwide increase of temperature would be abated if everyone, including you and me, used their car less. According to German research, road vehicles emit 155 times more carbon dioxide per passenger-kilometre than a train. Market estimates suggest that we are on the verge of a car boom, with car and truck sales reaching 74.7 million units a year worldwide compared with 49.3 million today. It is estimated that in Britain alone sales will jump from the present 1.6 million units a year to 2.7 million units by 2010. The UK roads are among the most congested in Europe; but the predictions point to a rise from the present 25.2 million cars on our roads to 34 million during that period – unless restraints are introduced.

Cars run on precious fossil fuels, and when we waste fossil fuels we are depleting world resources which took millions and millions of years to create. You may be thinking: Why, then, don't we run our cars on electricity? Even if we did, most electricity is generated from fossil fuels. Or you may be thinking: Why don't we find an alternative fuel? Some countries use methanol made out of alcohol, but that is no answer in a world hungry for food. Perhaps in the distant future cars may be able to run on liquid hydrogen, but nobody can at present find any way of producing this at anywhere near an economic price, and then making it a safe fuel for driving. I know that compared with the fires that raged in the oil wells of Kuwait, the amount of petrol used in my car or yours may seem infinitesimal. But multiply that by 400 million cars in use today, and you see what bad stewardship it is to waste this valuable fossil fuel. God gives us resources to use, not to squander. In the end the use of fossil fuels in our motor cars is a matter of our accountability before God for the use of his gifts in creation.

ACTION NEEDED

So what can be done about it? Lots and lots of things. Governments can take action, for example by improving public transport and by introducing disincentives for driving on the roads – such as reducing taxes on cars and increasing them on petrol (although in the past an increase in petrol prices has scarcely affected road mileage).

I am not concerned here with public measures, because without the goodwill of individual people they will not be very effective. And so I ask: What can we do ourselves individually? We can do a very great deal. If we have a car, we can see that its engine is small and efficient, so that it will use less petrol. We can use public transport whenever we can do so without undue inconvenience. We can buy a car that can run on unleaded petrol, and to which a catalytic converter can be fitted. We can share each other's cars if they are used for going to work: at present, we see long queues of cars with only a single occupant. And we can try to prevent ourselves driving like Jehu. I have to confess to my shame that I have had several convictions for speeding, so I am preaching to myself as much as to you. I also have to report with shame that, in our fallen world, my speeding fines actually helped to make me popular among the Brummies! May God forgive all our pasts, and help us to do better in the future!

10
WATER

He sendeth the springs into the valleys, which run among the hills.
They give drink to every beast of the field: the wild asses quench
their thirst. . . . O Lord, how manifold are thy works! in wisdom
hast thou made them all: the earth is full of thy riches. So is this
great and wide sea, wherein are things creeping innumerable, both
small and great beasts.

PSALM 104.10–11, 24–25 (AV)

What a blessing water is! It refreshes and revives us. It is life-giving,
enabling seeds to fertilize in the soil. It washes us and cleanses us.
Children love playing with water, adults like swimming in water –
perhaps at one stage of evolution our forebears were aquatic apes. It is
wonderfully recycled by nature. Moisture evaporates from the oceans
into the skies, and then comes down again to earth in the form of rain
or snow. Most of this drains into rivers which return it to the sea.
Evolution itself could not have taken place without water. It was in
the waters that life most probably first evolved. Water is such a blessing that it is hardly surprising that it is a universal religious symbol.
We find it used in this sense in the New Testament. In St John's
gospel, Jesus promises spiritual water which will be like a fountain
welling up to eternal life. We are baptized in the waters of the font,
which symbolize on the one hand the waters of the womb in which we
received life and, on the other hand, the waters of death which drown
us so that we may rise to life eternal.

PROVIDENCE AND WATER

How providential that water still abounds on our planet, when it has
disappeared from the others! Originally Venus may have had up to a
third as much water as Planet Earth. Probably life itself helped the
earth to retain its water. Photosynthesis through the leaves of plants
converts carbon dioxide into carbon and two atoms of oxygen, and
two atoms of oxygen in turn combine with one of hydrogen to make

water, H_2O. While hydrogen gas could escape into outer space, hydrogen locked up in water is too heavy to do this. So, in the providence of God, water itself contributes to the maintenance of life.

Nobody knows how the oceans were formed. After all, we are talking about a period some 4 billion years ago! Possibly the oceans were there before land appeared. More probably, the oceans derived from the earth's interior after the planet had accreted. The oceans' water is salty, marvellously and providentially preserved over the millennia at around its present level of 3.4 per cent salt (by weight), and it can never have risen above 6 per cent, beyond which few organisms can survive. We take the oceans for granted. In Britain we live on an island – 'this precious stone set in the silver sea' – and so for us the ocean is a barrier, a form of protection. We know that it is the source of valuable food, but it exists for us at the periphery of life and not at its centre. When we think of our planet, we think primarily of land, of the five continents, and then only secondarily of the oceans that separate them.

But if we are to think ecologically we need to make a great act of the imagination. Our planet should logically be called not the Earth, but the Ocean, for the seas take up seven-tenths of its surface. Naturally the impact of the oceans on the planet as a whole is enormous. Water evaporates from the oceans, and water vapour keeps the earth warm, before it comes down again as rain to fertilize the earth. The oceans and the atmosphere are interdependent: together they determine the patterns of climate around the globe. There are powerful currents conveying warmer water into colder areas, without which, for example, the climate of northern Europe (including Britain) would be arctic. Beneath the surface of the oceans the vast masses of placid water stabilize the climate. They also absorb vast amounts of various gases. Without the oceans for example, and their ability to absorb carbon dioxide, the greenhouse effect would have been apparent long before now.

Compared with the diameter of the globe as a whole, the oceans are only like a moist film smeared over its surface. All the same, there are tremendous variations, from gently sloping continental shelves near the landmasses to chasms and abysses deeper than Mount Everest is high. Down in the deepest oceans it is pitch dark and nearly freezing; but thousands of species of fish inhabit these depths. Vast amounts of minerals lie on the ocean bed waiting to be harvested. There are ocean valleys and ocean plains. Just as on earth there is the Sahara as well as tropical forests, so in the oceans there are sandy stretches and areas of intense habitation, especially on continental shelves and estuaries. The areas of the oceans which are most rich in life lie off the coasts:

the mangrove swamps and coral reefs of the tropical areas, and the saltmarshes and estuaries of the more temperate zones. Here flourish the living things that constitute the start of the food chain, plankton, small one-celled organisms not unlike life as it first evolved. Phytoplankton capture the energy of the sun and turn it into food and oxygen. These provide pasture for zooplankton, microscopic animals which form food for larger animals. The food chain leads from them right up to the chief predator of all, *Homo sapiens*, who, through overfishing (especially with the use of drift nets which are indiscriminate in their destruction) and through pollution, is now threatening the continuing health of the oceans.

POLLUTION OF THE OCEANS

How do we pollute the oceans? What happens in coastal waters is worse than in the deep oceans. Nutrients flowing down rivers can cause what are called 'eutrophic' conditions in which phytoplankton multiply and bloom. They can suffocate fish by preventing them from getting oxygen. Sometimes they are poisonous, and warnings have to be given against eating shellfish from the area. Untreated sewage may be discharged into the sea near coastal towns. This not only makes bathing filthy, but positively dangerous. Chemical works are permitted to dump large quantities of toxic materials into the sea. We all know the hazards of oil slicks, and the dangers that these cause for fish and birds. Some synthetic compounds are long lasting and do not break down in sea water. We have all heard of DDT and PCBs. In the 1970s these were identified as the cause of spontaneous abortions and premature births of sea-lions in California! Many other products enter the sea through rivers as run-off from agricultural land, or from municipal discharges. There is a particularly nasty product called TBT, which was deliberately used in boat anti-fouling paints, especially in marinas, and which caused gross malformation of oysters and other fish. The use of TBT for small boats has now been prohibited in Britain. Metals can also pollute the oceans. These build up in phytoplankton, and some of them also in fish. You may have heard of the disaster caused by mercury from paper mills in Minimata Bay in Japan, for which compensatory payments are still being made. As a result, many countries introduced controls, but around estuaries there can still be high levels of metals.

One cause for anxiety is the dumping of radio-active waste in the oceans. Although it is said to be safe, no one can really know how long the containers will remain sealed, and if the wastes leak we are leaving in the ocean bed a kind of toxic time bomb for posterity. Fortunately, Britain has recently discontinued this practice.

One of the greatest causes of pollution is the persistent litter in the high seas, especially plastic. Just imagine the national beach clean-up in the USA in 1988 which removed nearly a thousand tons of debris from 2,000 miles of shoreline! Some 62 per cent of this litter was plastic. In the high seas plastic litter comes from fishing gear, packaging materials, and 'convenience items': it finds its way to the remotest areas. It can cause the death of wildlife either through entanglement or through ingestion. To give you some idea of the problem, you might be interested to know that in the North Pacific 30,000 northern fur seals are estimated to be dying annually from entanglement in lost or discarded fish gear, and some 60,000 animals are similarly killed off the Norwegian coast. Nobody knows the long-term effect of these pollutants on immune systems. For example, a virus infection recently killed 18,000 seals in the North Sea and the Baltic, but it was suspected that pollution in the North Sea had weakened their immune systems.

Those seas most at risk seem to be those that are near the great centres of industrial activity. The North Sea is one such. There, traces of many effluents from rivers are to be found, but the most disturbing, ecologically speaking, are the algal blooms that result from 'eutrophication' when a high level of nutrients in the water encourages the algae to multiply wildly. Spectacular blooms have occurred. One of the plagues was to turn the Nile blood-red, but off the Scandinavian coast the same phenomenon has appeared on a far vaster scale, killing many salmon and recalling the words of Lady Macbeth about 'the multitudinous seas incarnadine, making the green one red'. The Mediterranean Sea, an almost land-locked area with no tides, is also polluted; it has high coastal populations and some 100 million tourists each year. There are algal blooms, deterioration of fish stocks, and evidence of industrial pollution; and the scenarios expected for 2025 show that a worsening must be expected unless more rigorous measures are taken than those presently in force. If you are a tourist and make your way in the summer to the Mediterranean sunshine, you will be well aware of the threat to the waters of this delectable area. Other areas of sea are similarly affected: part of the North Atlantic coastline, the oceans surrounding Japan, and the Pacific Coast. The oceans are under threat.

RIVERS

Most – but not all – of the pollution that reaches the sea comes to it down the rivers. This means that rivers are also polluted, and polluted with the same substances as those which pollute the oceans. People have always used rivers for drinking water supplies, as sewers, for food and for transport, and as waste dumps. Nowadays we have sophisticated technology, but the primary uses still remain. Agriculture produces nitrates, phosphates and slurry; industry produces chemical waste, accidental spillage, oil and acid rain; you and I may contribute indirectly with sewage effluent, litter and dumping; building construction contributes effluence and increased sediment. Surely, you may think, that list is complete. Oh no, it's not. We have forgotten what drains off the roads: de-icing salt, oil and heavy metals. Of course, the list is actually far longer than this. The trouble is that if the pollution enters the river near its source, its whole length is affected.

However, Britain has a National Rivers Authority, which is concerned with the management of our rivers, the abstraction of water and water pollution, and shortly we shall have an Environmental Protection Agency. In any case, the health of our rivers has greatly increased over the last 30 years. But the same cannot be said of our drinking water. There are three main concerns. There are apparent links between small amounts of aluminium in our drinking water and Alzheimer's disease, a form of senile dementia. Many old water pipes are made of lead, and there is fear that ingestion of this lead may affect the intellectual development of children; and, despite what the experts say, there are unknown risks presented by the vast number of chemicals, including pesticides, released into the environment by water. These risks are unknown because they are recent, and they may present a cumulative hazard. We do now have the legal right to find out what is in our tap water, and the privatized supplier has to give us this information free of charge; but because the British Government had sanctioned standards below those demanded by the European Community, the Friends of the Earth actually had to begin legal proceedings to ensure the required quality of water. Other rivers in Europe are not all as good as ours. I recently sailed all the way down the Rhine. I would not have liked to bathe in its soupy waters, or to eat fish caught in it, where they can be caught. But at least it is much better than it used to be. And industrial nations are becoming aware of what is needed, as the report of the OECD (the Organisation for Economic Co-operation and Development) makes crystal clear. But as yet there is no International Oceans Authority other than the United

Nations, and we need to hope and pray that this will be more effective in conserving the fish and animals who live in our oceans, and in protecting their ecosystems on which so much depends.

★ ★ ★

Now that we are more aware of what is happening, the situation is likely to get better. There is no cause for pessimism. And whilst we have to think about water pollution, let us not forget that water is a marvellous gift from God. As St Francis of Assisi's Canticle reminds us:

> Thou flowing water, pure and clear,
> Make music for thy Lord to hear,
> Alleluiah, alleluiah.

11

ACID RAIN

*Then the Lord rained upon Sodom and upon Gomorrah brimstone
and fire from the Lord out of heaven; And he overthrew those
cities, and all the plain, and all the inhabitants of the cities, and
that which grew upon the ground.*

GENESIS 19.24–25 (AV)

You may think that it is a bit far fetched to start a sermon on acid rain
with a text about Sodom and Gomorrah, for the two are very different
indeed. And yet there is one very strange similarity. The cause of the
explosion which has obliterated all trace of those settlements near the
Dead Sea which flourished in the days of Abraham and Lot probably
has much in common with the cause of acid rain. Let me read you an
extract from the commentary on the Book of Genesis by the famous
Old Testament scholar Gerhard von Rad:

> It is quite possible that the tradition contains a distant recollection
> of an actual catastrophe. Perhaps a tectonic earthquake released
> gases (hydrogen sulphide) or opened up the way for asphalt and
> petroleum. If these minerals were ignited, 'it would be easy for the
> entire mass of air over the opened chasm to be suddenly in flames'.
> As a matter of fact, the Dead Sea coastal area today is rich in
> deposits of asphalt and sulphur.

If this explanation is correct, and there was sulphur in the atmosphere, then when it next rained in that area – and this does not often
happen now – there would have been a form of acid rain.

However, acid rain today has a different origin. It results from
combustion, but not in the open air. Its effect is not so immediate,
although, as we shall see, the damage quickly escalates. 40 per cent is
caused by the processes of nature, the rest by the actions of human
beings, through their burning of fossil fuels or their factory emissions.
And so the destruction which acid rain causes is not the direct result
of God's punishment of human wickedness, in the way that Genesis
records, but rather it inevitably happens when human beings upset
the balances of nature which keep our atmosphere comfortable for
life. In that sense, it can indeed be called a judgement upon us. It was

56

one matter when we upset this balance unwittingly, but now that we know what we are doing and have the power to put things right, we are far more directly to blame.

WHAT IS ACID RAIN?

First of all, what does the phrase 'acid rain' mean? It has nothing to do with a drug epidemic or anything like that. The words are commonly used to cover all forms of acid deposition, be it from gas or mist or in dry form. Sulphur in a gaseous form is emitted naturally by algae, and so rain is naturally acidic, but only very mildly so. Emissions of sulphur dioxide and nitrogen oxides greatly contribute to this acidity – 70 per cent in the case of sulphur dioxide and 30 per cent in the case of nitrogen oxide. Some 71 per cent of the sulphur emissions come from power stations, most of which burn coal. As for the nitrogen oxides, road transport accounts for nearly a half, power stations for a third, and the rest comes from industry. Obviously, once these pollutants are airborne, they can be carried for long distances – for example from Eastern Europe to Scandinavia. As for pollution, Britain exports far more than it imports! Only 20 per cent comes to us from overseas. The rest we make ourselves. Although Britain is not the worst in the acid rain table – Eastern Europe is worse – it is certainly the dirty man of the European Community so far as acid rain is concerned.

What effect does this form of pollution have? The answer to that question is: a great many. The first may affect you. The sulphur and nitrogen compounds can affect human beings and result in breathing problems. Ozone, too, which is formed through the interaction of nitrogen oxides with sunlight, is also bad for us down here, though essential up in the ozone layer. Sometimes in Britain the levels of sulphur dioxide and nitrogen oxides have exceeded the guidelines laid down by the World Health Organization, especially in areas of heavy traffic or near coal-fired power stations. People who cycle tend to wear masks nowadays, but I am told that they do very little good. The levels must come down.

Secondly, the pollution affects trees. And it can happen quite quickly. For example, a research officer of the Forestry Commission in England visited Germany in 1982, and the damage he found there in trees was almost entirely confined to the mountains. Only a year later, in 1983, he found to his great surprise that 40 per cent of the total forest area had been affected. In 1987 a German research officer

57

warned that 'Waldsterben' (as it is called there) could be 'the beginning of the greatest ecological catastrophe which ever took place'. You may well ask, how could that have happened? The answer is that deposition levels had passed a critical level. As I have said before, the controls that operate in our ecosystems are very elastic but when elastic is overstretched it collapses. That was what happened in Germany. You will probably have heard how badly the Black Forest has been affected.

This painful discovery about Germany prompted this research officer to consider the position in Britain. It was a complex operation, the first such survey to be attempted, and there are always good years and bad years for trees, depending on the weather and other factors. You need to look out for the height of a tree, its diameter, the yellowing of the crown, the browning of the needles in conifers, and other factors. The latest survey about Britain came from the United Nations in 1989. It showed that 28 per cent of British trees surveyed showed moderate to severe defoliation. When I first read about this report, I refused to believe it! The trees around my house appear to be in good health. So I decided to keep a lookout, especially in Forestry Commission plantations near the border of Wales. I was horrified at what I saw. On many conifers there was no foliage at the top of the trees. This is something quite separate from Dutch Elm disease, or the assaults that have been made on beeches. It was due predominantly to acid rain.

Acid rain also affects life in surface waters. Norway has reported that all of the lakes in an area covering 13,000 square kilometres are now devoid of fish. When the pollution reaches a critical stage the snails and invertebrates that the fish eat cannot survive, the fish eggs cannot hatch and the fry are killed. The fish themselves may be killed by the acidity of the water, or they may suffocate because their gills become clogged through the concentration of aluminium which is permitted by the acidity of the water. In Britain, the Central Electricity Board, way back in 1986, admitted the link between power-station emissions and acidified lakes in southern Scandinavia. But subsequent research has shown that only 15 per cent comes from Britain. I wonder whether you are aware that rivers in western and central Scotland, the Lake District, the Pennines and the Welsh uplands are now affected? When our children were young, we used to take our holidays in central Wales, and there was marvellous trout fishing in the streams. I went back there a few years ago to open a small nature reserve, and I found to my horror that the streams are now dead.

Acid rain also affects drinking water and crops, although in a rather different way. The acidification of water can sometimes be accompanied by an increase in aluminium. If a causal relationship between aluminium and Alzheimer's disease is confirmed, this can have serious consequences if the water is used by humans for drinking purposes. Soil acidity may in future contribute to concentrations in food of the highly toxic metal cadmium. Although sulphur and nitrogen oxides at present levels are unlikely to affect agriculture, ozone, which is formed in sunlight by interaction with nitrogen oxides, is likely in some areas to reduce crop yields.

There is one further aspect of acid rain pollution that I must mention. Sulphur dioxide is a major pollutant so far as buildings are concerned, and especially ancient buildings. Churchgoers have to find millions of pounds for the maintenance of their cathedrals and parish churches which they hold in trust. In 1990 a report in Britain suggested that building maintenance expenditure could be substantially reduced if a 30 per cent reduction of levels of ambient sulphur dioxide were carried out. It was even suggested that the costs of reducing these emissions would be unlikely to exceed the savings made in maintenance expenditure. But then different people have to find the money – in the one case, the government or the power companies, and in the other, the voluntary contributions of church people and well-wishers.

ATTEMPTS TO REDUCE POLLUTION

Clearly the level of these sulphur and nitrogen emissions must be curtailed. Since their effects cross national frontiers, action on an international scale is needed. In 1985 the USA and Britain refused to sign the Helsinki Protocol for a 30 per cent reduction in sulphur dioxide emissions, and in 1988 Britain also refused to join with twelve other countries in an informal 30 per cent 'nitrogen oxide club'. The most it would do was to join the Sofia Protocol, which agreed to a standstill by 1994 in nitrogen oxide emissions at a 1987 baseline.

In 1984 the European Community finally agreed an air directive. It took five years to agree, largely because of objections on the part of Britain. The former Chief Scientist and Deputy Secretary to the Department of the Environment admitted in 1989 that British policy in the 1970s and 1980s suffered from 'conspicuous weaknesses' and showed 'an arrogant dismissal of overseas experience and expertise'. When agreement in the European Community was finally reached, this was not achieved on the basis of targets and goals so much as

59

economics and costs. Different countries agreed to different limitations on emissions. The UK government, in the words of the EC Commissioner, 'obtained their relatively undemanding limits on the understanding that the UK would achieve the required reductions chiefly through FGD'. These initials stand for Flue Gas Desulphurization by means of the fitting of devices through which limestone and gypsum is sprayed at the smoke before it is released into the open air. Although it is claimed that there are better methods than this, it is agreed to be 95 per cent effective. The British government agreed to spend £2 billion on fitting this equipment on six of the large power stations. However, in 1990 the government reneged on this commitment, confining its plans to only three power stations, and arguing that further commitment would be 'inappropriate'. It is left to the privatized power companies to reduce pollution further either by using coal with less sulphur content, or through the use of natural gas, or through fitting their own desulphurization equipment.

This story is not a happy one. I have tried to give it to you straight, without passing any political judgements, because I believe that this is inappropriate in a sermon. Perhaps I should add that, taking 1980 emissions as a baseline, the UK has agreed to a progressive reduction in emissions of nitrogen oxides and sulphur dioxide; the latter reducing by 20 per cent by 1993 leading to 60 per cent by 2003. A review may be made in 1994. The European Community has also insisted that by 1992 all new cars will be fitted with catalytic converters, which will greatly help the elimination of nitrogen oxide emissions.

* * *

I apologize if I have become too technical. It is only too easy for a sermon on a subject like this to become a lecture. But we cannot dispense with the facts! And there is a profound moral point here. Remember Sodom and Gomorrah! We must pay not only for the goods and services which we buy, but also for the cost of eliminating the pollution which these produce. But if you feel the need to urge faster action against acid rain on the part of the government, don't expect the Church to act. It is not here for that purpose. Join an environmental agency which will help you to do this. And each one of us can assist by using less electricity, and by ensuring that our car, if it is not a new one, is fitted, if possible, with a catalytic converter.

12

AGRICULTURE

*For the Lord thy God bringeth thee into a good land, a land of
brooks of water, of fountains and depths that spring out of valleys
and hills; a land of wheat, and barley, and vines, and fig trees, and
pomegranates; a land of oil olive, and honey; a land wherein thou
shalt eat bread without scarceness, thou shalt not lack any thing in
it . . .*

DEUTERONOMY 8.7–9 (AV)

What delight that promise still conjures up for us today, some 2,000
years after it is said to have been given! What a paradisal scene, what a
picture of plenitude and plenty, a kind of combination of Constable
country with Wordsworthian wonderland! No wonder it inspired the
Israelites on their desert wanderings, when their soul had 'dried away'
and they only had manna to eat and they were pining for the cucum-
bers, the melons, the leeks, the onions and the garlic of Egypt! The
ancient world, with its rural economy, depended totally upon the rain
and the rivers and the springs, and barren land meant poverty and
even starvation. Admittedly, Deuteronomy gives us a somewhat exaggerated account of the fertility of the Promised Land, but in such a
situation a little overstatement is readily forgiven. This promise of the
good land is deeply engraved on the folk memory of the Jews, and it
accounts in part for Israel's insistence on regaining and retaining the
land promised to them of old.

FOOD IN ABUNDANCE

And today, what do we find? Has this promise, given to the Jews,
proved to be universal for all humanity? When we go into the supermarkets and see all the profusion of foods offered there for us to buy,
it might seem that it has. When we hear of all the grain that has to be
put into store under the Common Agricultural Policy, or the amount
of agricultural land that is 'set aside', and when we actually look out
on the British landscape, from the train or from the road, and we see

acre after acre of flourishing crops of wheat or barley, or orchards and soft fruit, it might seem that this is the case. Paradise seems to have arrived. And yet a little enquiry will make it clear to us that only 1 billion out of the 5½ billion inhabitants of the world share in this prosperity, and in any case the fertility which makes it possible is short-lived and precarious. All is not well.

Wonderful strides have been made in agricultural science, so that far greater yields are now possible compared with the days of old – although even then 'some thirtyfold, some sixtyfold and some a hundredfold' seems to have been possible. Yet this very success brings with it some dangers. Nowadays people tend only to grow the crop which brings the greatest yield. But we badly need genetic variety and biological diversity. For if the climate and the temperature change – and global warming threatens just this – other forms of grain and plants will be needed. They need to be preserved. It is good that genetic material of both plants and animals is being preserved in deep freezes.

FERTILIZERS

The soil has always needed fertilizers. In the past, natural fertilizers from animal wastes have been used. But the recent huge yields of grain have only been possible through the application of masses and masses of artificial fertilizers and through very thorough spraying with artificial pesticides. This is the worry. Some 30 kilograms per person per crop is applied each year in order to obtain these yields. Think of the amount of fossil fuels that is used to obtain all this fertilizer! Granted it may increase the crop, but it does not improve the soil, and increasing amounts will be necessary in order to maintain the yield, making the soil deteriorate further.

It is true that farmers today often deny the bad effect that artificial fertilizers have on the soil. However, there is now proof that this does happen. A very interesting experiment was carried out recently when a comparison of the soil was made on two identical and neighbouring farms in the eastern part of Washington State in the USA: one of the farms used artificial fertilizers and pesticides and the other used organic methods. The report is unambiguous:

Though the two fields in this study have the same type of soil and were probably identical 40 years ago, the topsoil is now eroding more rapidly on the conventional field. At this rate all the topsoil on typical Naff and similar soils under conventional farming systems will be lost in another 50 to 100 years. When this happens, the yields from these soils could drop by one third or more. The organic farmer should be able to maintain the topsoil for generations to come, although he could slow the rate of erosion still further by adopting other practices to conserve the soil.

When we did not know what we were doing, conventional farming practice was excusable. But now we do know. We are knowingly using up one of the world's most precious inheritances, which has taken thousands and thousands of years to form: the precious topsoil which gives fertility to plant life. We have surely no right to deprive posterity of this precious resource, which should be entailed on all future generations. It may seem that we are now enjoying a fertility like that which was promised to the Israelites of old; but it is literally an *artificial fertility*, and one which generations to come will curse us for enjoying.

But, you may well ask, what yields would we get if organic methods of farming were generally adopted? Granted, it may seem more moral; but is it even feasible? Will we all go hungry as a result? The use of artificial fertilizers has increased from a world total of 14 million tons in 1950 to an estimated 143 million tons in 1980! But some of this has not really been necessary. For example, nitrogen is applied to the soil, but researchers have recently discovered that if clover is planted alongside cereals, it not only fertilizes the crop but also protects it from pests. Nonetheless, it has been estimated that if the use of artificial fertilizers suddenly came to an end, there would be a catastrophic drop of 40 per cent in crop yields. Farmers would have to learn the art of using organic fertilizers again. Land which is farmed organically, without artificial fertilizers and pesticides, *can* be just as productive as land pumped full of chemicals. It produces slightly less food, certainly, but the food is of a higher quality. If it were not so, organic farmers would not be able to make a living. This is the way farming is going today. An increasing number of people prefer organically farmed food not for reasons of ecology, but because they prefer the taste and the texture, and they are worried about the long-term effects of artificial fertilizers and pesticides on their own health.

OTHER EFFECTS OF FERTILIZERS

Apart from the soil, what other effects do fertilizers have? Nitrates can sink into the water table, and find their way into drinking water. This takes a long time to happen, and therefore any controls which are introduced similarly take a long time to be effective. When nitrates are ingested by human beings they can turn into nitrites which are toxic. There are limits beyond which nitrates are not allowed to pollute our water, but already in some places these limits are breached. What will happen if increasing amounts of nitrates have to be used in order to sustain high yields? I think we all know the answer to that. Fortunately, some action is being taken by designating some areas as Nitrate Sensitive Areas, where the use of artificial fertilizers can be regulated. Another effect that artificial fertilizers can have is what is called 'eutrophication' in our rivers. The fertilizers get washed into the rivers and encourage algae to multiply, producing surface scum. The lack of oxygen which results can have a disastrous effect on the fish and other living things in the rivers. I expect many of us have seen some evidence of this for ourselves.

There is one kind of fertilizer in very general use which comes from a natural source, and which also causes eutrophication: I refer to phosphates. These are not only used for agriculture, but they are also found in detergents that are not 'environmentally friendly'. Phosphates are dug from large deposits of guano, a natural manure found in great abundance on some sea coasts, and especially on the islands around Peru. It is formed from the massed droppings of sea birds, and the phosphate comes from the fish which they catch in the oceans. There has evolved a natural system of recycling phosphates by this means, but this has been interrupted by the use of this material as a fertilizer on the land. What will happen when all the guano is used up? Posterity will have to do without it.

PESTICIDES

As for pesticides, they are very necessary if we are to grow food successfully. A constant war has to be waged against the insects that thrive on the things we grow. It is reckoned that without pesticides 30 per cent of the crop would be lost before harvesting it. However, it is easy to kill an insect, without realizing that by so doing we might be killing the predator of a worse kind of pest! The last state of affairs would be worse than the first. Agriculturalists have by now learnt their lesson here. There are two kinds of pesticides, those which come from natural sources (and which are generally safe) and those which are manufactured. A careful watch has to be kept on the latter, for they are potentially dangerous. Some of them have to be sprayed on plants with great care, and residues may remain on foodstuffs if they are not carefully washed before they are used. Some of the pesticides seem to move around the planet very easily, blown by the winds. Traces of DDT were even found near the North Pole! This is a very technical area, into which I do not intend to enter, except to say that, despite government assurances about maximum residue levels and the existence of government advisory committees, there are many informed people who worry a great deal not only about the effects of these pesticides on those whose job it is to administer them, but also about the long-term effects which the residues may have on those who consume the foods on which they have been sprayed.

IRRIGATION

Successful agriculture today needs more than artificial fertilizers and pesticides. High-yielding seeds are also required, and these have been produced by the skills and knowledge of agricultural scientists; and no doubt the new biotechnology, with the artificial insertion of genes, will help still more. Also needed are very large supplies of water. Farming accounts for about 70 per cent of all water that is used on the planet! About a third of the world's crops come from irrigated farmland. This century there has been an enormous increase in irrigation: from some 50 million hectares in 1900 to 250 million hectares today. Much of this irrigated water, however, does not benefit the farmer: some 40 per cent is wasted. Bad irrigation actually causes harm, creating barren land by washing salts to the surface: that is how the deserts around the Euphrates were caused. Many large-scale barrages have now been built, and it seems as though we are reaching the limits of irrigation. In any case, the vast amount of annual water abstraction from the rivers of the world – six times the annual flow of the Mississippi – is causing a decline in the reserves of water beneath the soil, waterlogged and salted land, and shrinking lakes and inland seas. Droughts can now have catastrophic effects. There will be further problems if and when the 'greenhouse effect' becomes more obvious. As the climate changes, irrigation is unlikely to be able to afford the degree of crop protection and yield enhancement which the world comes to expect, and which its growing population will need.

★ ★ ★

At the beginning of this sermon, I said that the degree of plenty which this planet now enjoys is fragile. You will know what I meant. If God's promise given to the ancient Jews now seems to have been universalized, it is unlikely to be enjoyed by those who come after us. Once again we must look to the future. We are guardians of the soil, its fertility and its healthiness. We are accountable to God. We must ensure that we do not leave a barren and unhealthy soil to those who come after us. We must ensure that by our agriculture we do not disrupt the essential ecosystems of the planet. And yet we feel so helpless. But in reality we are masters of our fate. If we so wish, we can show our convictions politically. We could join the green lobby. We are all consumers, and consumers are in a very strong position. We can ask questions about the food we buy, and we can refuse to buy what is environmentally bad. What we must not do, if we profess to be Christian, is to shrug our shoulders and say none of this is our business. It is. We are responsible for the good land God has given us.

13
LIVESTOCK

*Blessed shall be the fruit of thy body, and the fruit of thy ground,
and the fruit of thy cattle, the increase of thy kine, and the flocks
of thy sheep.*

DEUTERONOMY 28.4 (AV)

At first sight it might seem as though that blessing once given to the
ancient Jews has now been fulfilled worldwide. There are now some
5½ billion people alive on the planet. But did you know that domesticated animals now outnumber human beings by three to one? The
planet now holds over 2 billion four-legged livestock and 11 billion
fowls! There has been a dramatic upsurge in production in the recent
past. Within 40 years, meat production has almost quadrupled! A
biologist has observed that 'an alien ecologist, observing the earth,
might conclude that cattle is the dominant animal species in our biosphere'. Cattle and other livestock such as pigs and poultry graze one-
half of the planet's total land area. 'And why not?' you may well ask.
If it can be produced, why shouldn't people eat as much meat as they
can afford? Humanity is not vegetarian by nature. Most people enjoy
their roast beef or pork chop. According to the Scriptures, human
beings, after the Flood, were allowed to eat the flesh of beasts and
birds. Surely God is 'green'? Are the environmentalists really going to
try to stop us enjoying what Scripture expressly allows?

CHANGES IN PASTORAL PRACTICE

One of primitive humanity's greatest achievements was to domesticate
the buffalo and so to breed cattle. What a variety of needs they used to
meet! They provided food, fuel, fertilizer, transport and clothing. In
some primitive countries they still constitute the main form of transport, and in rural India, where cows are sacred, their wastes still
provide a third of the total fuel energy. Manure is valuable in sustain-
ing the fertility of the soil. Did you know that in India a farmer will
get more money for his goat manure than he will for his goats' milk?

But in developed countries, crop rotation, including grazing, has given way to the use of artificial fertilizers to sustain arable crops. In the old days, animals turned what people could not eat into things people could; cattle and sheep would eat grass while pigs and fowl would eat crop wastes, kitchen scraps, and whatever else they could find. Nowadays, animals in the West are fed grain and are often bred intensively. As a result, mountains of manure, especially pig manure, are piling up in some countries like the Netherlands, and as yet no one can find a way to dispose of it. If you have ever been downwind from an intensive pig farm, you will have smelled out what I mean! Livestock is now produced in the West almost entirely for human consumption, and in undeveloped countries, where the poor are often pastoralists, pressure of population has forced people to put on the land more cattle than it can support. This has affected the whole balance of nature worldwide. If you think that this sounds like a bit of an exaggeration, let me tell you how the situation appears by quoting the Worldwatch Institute in Washington:

> Rings of barren earth spread out from the wells on the grasslands of Southern Turkmenia. Heather and lilies wilt in the nature preserves of the Southern Netherlands. Forests teeming with rare forms of life explode in flame in Costa Rica. Water tables fall and fossil fuels are wasted in the United States. Each of these cases of environmental decline issues from a single source: the global livestock industry.

We who live in towns tend to be rather sentimental about cattle being reared in the countryside. We may recall Gray's *Elegy Written in a Country Churchyard*:

> The curfew tolls the knell of parting day,
> The lowing herd winds slowly o'er the lea . . .

But Gray wrote in the eighteenth century. The position near the end of the twentieth century is very different. The situation is bad, whether we live in the impoverished Third World or the developed worlds of North America and the European Community.

THIRD WORLD PRESSURES

Much of the pasture in the Third World is drylands. The pressure of population means that more livestock is grazed on the land – the population of the Sahel for example has doubled. The cattle eat the

68

perennial grasses bare, so weeds and tougher shrubs spread in their place. Cattle tend to stamp down the soil, which then becomes permeable to rain, and so when it does rain the topsoil tends to be swept away and deep gullies formed. In countries like Botswana, bore holes are dug to give water; but the cattle are not controlled around these water holes, and so the earth around them becomes bare and infertile. This is all part of the process of 'desertification' which is said to have already affected a third of the world's 3 billion hectares of dry rangeland. This is what happens when this kind of country is overstocked. Another hazard in developing countries is the cutting down of forests in order to produce grazing land for cattle. In fact, such land is very poor and cannot support livestock for long. We hear a great deal nowadays about the loss of tropical forests, and rightly so. But we do not always realize that this has been caused by clearances in order to introduce livestock production. Within twenty years, 20 million hectares of tropical forest have been destroyed for farmers and ranchers, especially in Brazil, Bolivia and Colombia.

PRESSURES IN THE DEVELOPED WORLD

The story is rather different in the developed countries. Although the number of livestock at any one time is not so many as in developing countries, in fact the production is four times as large, because they do not live so long. This is because they put on weight very quickly because they are fed on grain, with the European Community the third largest consumer after the USA and the former USSR. Grain for livestock uses up a quarter of the world's croplands! Yet grain production is no longer keeping up with the world's increasing population. And this grain is produced in an energy-intensive way. For example, pigs consume more grain than any other meat industry, and in American pig production it takes the equivalent of 4 litres of petrol to produce a couple of pounds of pork!

The wastes from cattle intensively farmed also help to degrade the soil. In the Netherlands and elsewhere, more phosphorus and nitrogen from manure is produced than the soil can absorb. These can suffocate surface water with algae, and they can also percolate through to the water table, and nitrates from this and other sources may cause illnesses such as cancer. Nitrogen from manure escapes into the air as ammonia, and contributes to acid rain. In some areas, pollution from cattle causes more damage in this way than pollution from industry. And this is not all. It may sound indelicate to mention this in a sermon, but it is a fact of life that cattle produce methane gas. They release some 80 million tons of gas each year in belches and flatulence, and a further 35 million tons is produced from their wastes. Livestock account for 15–20 per cent of global methane emissions, which works out at 3 per cent of all 'greenhouse' gases. And this really does affect us all, because methane gas contributes to the ozone deficiency in the upper atmosphere and, even more importantly, it is a gas which contributes powerfully to global warming. Did you realize that so much of this global warming gas comes from the digestive tracts of livestock?

UNSUSTAINABLE DEVELOPMENT

I hope that I have not overburdened you with information in this sermon about the effects of livestock on the environment. I have tried to give you the facts, as without these we are not in a position to interpret them. It is clear from what I have said that the present rate of livestock production is unsustainable. It is clear that it is impossible to raise the meat consumption of developing countries so that it reaches that of the developed nations. At the moment, meat consumption in the USA runs at 112 kilograms a person a year, while that of India is only 2 kilograms. Eastern Europe has a tradition of high consumption. The European Community consumes some 71 kilograms a year per person. Clearly, these amounts are unsustainable without causing continuing damage to the world environment. In other words, if we are to conserve the planet for those who come after us, we shall all have to eat less meat. Already there are trends towards this in Britain, partly because there are more vegetarians, partly because of the price of meat, and partly because people are beginning to realize that too much meat can be bad for our health.

Here, however, let us simply remind ourselves of our duty to God. God has made us trustees of this planet. There is no reason why we should not enjoy eating meat, but there is every reason for us to restrict meat consumption so that it no longer causes environmental damage. Trustees must not abuse their trust. 'It is required in stewards that a man be found faithful.'

14

RECYCLING

*And not many days after the younger son gathered all together, and
took his journey into a far country, and there wasted his substance
with riotous living.*

LUKE 15.13 (AV)

What on earth has the parable of the Prodigal Son got to do with
matters of the environment? It is not about the environment at all, but
about forgiveness. This is, after all, one of the very best known of all
Jesus' parables. The Prodigal Son asked for his inheritance while his
father was still alive, and then 'wasted his substance with riotous
living'. And then, after finding that he had nothing on which to live,
he returned to his father and asked to be one of his hired servants –
and he got a wonderful welcome. We naturally apply that parable to
feckless, selfish individuals, because it was told about a particular
person who did not take seriously what had been entrusted to him.

INDUSTRIAL SOCIETY AND THE PRODIGAL SON

But think of the story in connection with industrialized culture, and
you will find that it is a very exact parable of what we are doing in the
Western world. There is no need to 'journey into a far country': we
only have to look around us. In our present throwaway society, that is
precisely what we are doing: wasting our substance in riotous living.
We are acting as though there were limitless resources in this world,
just as the Prodigal Son acted as though he had limitless resources in
the world in which he lived. The son at least had to ask his father for
his share of his inheritance: we just grab the inheritance of posterity
and use it up in riotous living. However, you will recall that the
parable has a happy ending. The Prodigal Son came to his senses –
just in time. He returned penitent to his father, who welcomed him
from afar. The industrialized world too can come to its senses – just in
time – and return to our heavenly Father who will also welcome
us with open arms. The only trouble with this scenario is that the

71

industrialized world has not yet come to its senses, and at present shows few signs of returning to its heavenly Father; but there are at last some indications that 'the penny is beginning to drop'.

BUILT-IN OBSOLESCENCE

How do we waste 'our substance'? In the first place, there is a built-in obsolescence in many of the goods that we buy. Our light bulbs are so constructed that they will burn out after giving off so many hours of electric light – unless we use long-life ones. I have had some personal experience of this obsolescence during the last few months. First, my portable radio stopped working. I took it to the people who put these things right. 'I could do it for you, sir', the man said, 'but I have to warn you that it would be cheaper for you to buy a new one.' Then the family washing machine wouldn't work. The man who came to see it said: 'This model is over fifteen years old: we don't repair them as old as that'. I seem to have had a chapter of accidents lately, because shortly after this the family television set gave up. The man who came to see that said, 'This is eighteen years old: of course I can't repair it. It's only supposed to last for seven years.' There was a time when goods were built to last as long as possible, but repair work takes time and skill. Manufacture, which is now partly automated and requires few skills, is cheaper than repair, which does require skills. And, since our economic strategy is built on growth, this means that more and more goods have to be produced. These goods must not therefore last for too long, or people will not buy new ones. Fortunately, this view is not universal. The people of Sri Lanka know better. They are opening a factory to make the old Morris Minor car. They know it seems to last forever, because they still have original Morris Minors on their roads. In Britain, you are more likely to see such a vehicle in a museum for vintage cars.

PACKAGING

Again, goods are sold nowadays not only because of their excellence but because of their attractiveness. Packaging therefore becomes of enormous importance. Manufacturers have to see that their products are well packaged. And the wrappings are thrown away by those who buy the products. Just imagine for a moment that you are Mr Average

72

Man or Mrs Average Woman in Britain. Did you know that every year you will be throwing away the following: 90 drink cans, 107 bottles and jars, 45 kilograms of plastics, 70 food cans, 2 trees' worth of paper, 140 kilograms of food waste? We throw away each year as rubbish five times our own weight; altogether, 25 million tons of household and commercial rubbish. We don't realize how much trash there is until the dustmen go on strike! And further, there are all those industrial wastes that are dumped into pits, or thrown into the sea. We are quite right to get worried about wastes buried in landfill sites, because they not only use up land, but they can release globe-warming methane gas into the atmosphere and the wastes can leach into the groundwater – and if these are poisonous, they can do great harm. And wastes dumped into the sea can harm the living things in the oceans, which may in turn harm us or simply die out.

Well, it may seem surprising to you that you are accused of being like the Prodigal Son when you are leading a sober and sensible life. But I do hope that you can understand that from another point of view you are wasting 'our substance' and that of posterity 'in riotous living'. And of course I am as bad as you are. It's only we human beings who waste things in this way. Mother Nature takes care of discarded material when we don't interfere. We throw away things because we think that they are useless, but nature finds a use for natural leftovers. When animals die, they provide material for future generations. Organic material makes compost. Nutrients are recycled in the soil. Carbon dioxide is recycled through trees and plants. Recycling is essential for the health of the natural world. It's only human beings that leave waste lying around.

FIVE REASONS FOR CONSERVATION

Let me remind you of the reasons why we should not do this. First, we need to conserve for posterity valuable resources. Oil is an obvious example. But the same applies to metals. Reserves are limited. They are usually combined with other substances in crystalline, inorganic compounds. Refining these metals already uses enormous amounts of energy. Resources are different from reserves: the former word is used to describe the total amount of metal ores in the earth's crust, most of which are in such dilute concentrations that it is not economic to extract them. When conventional ores of precious metals are used up (what we call reserves), which is likely to be the case within the next half-century for some metals, then silicate metals will have to be broken down to extract further supplies. This will require from 100 to 1,000 times more energy than present processes. It is hard to see how it will ever be worth while, and substitute materials are more likely to be used.

A second reason for conserving materials is to save energy. Are you aware that 99 per cent of energy is saved on their manufacture if recycled polyethylene plastic is used rather than unrecycled? Did you know that if you read a newspaper printed on recycled paper, you are using material which uses only a quarter as much energy for its manufacture as it would require if unrecycled? Did you know that a recycled aluminium saucepan requires only 5 per cent of the energy to make it as a saucepan made from freshly mined bauxite? If you really want to help in cutting down energy use, here is a way of doing it: as far as is possible, use recycled goods.

Thirdly, throwaway material causes pollution. This follows from the smaller amount of energy used in recycling rather than making things from fresh material. Energy causes pollution. Throwaway material gets dumped in landfill sites and, as we have seen already, this can cause pollution.

Fourthly, there is the matter of preserving wildlife habitats. Materials like bauxite (for aluminium) often come from areas which used to be covered with rain forests. Finally, it is obviously cheaper to recycle now than to leave others to clean up our mess later.

RECENT MOVES TOWARDS RECYCLING

In Britain we are far behind many other countries in dealing with waste. We dump or burn 95 per cent of our rubbish, the highest proportion in Europe except for Greece. But improvements are on the way. In 1991 the EC issued an instruction to recycle 60 per cent of all packaging, rising to 90 per cent by the year 2000. Improvements are not always for environmental reasons: it is dawning on some that so far as waste is concerned, 'where there's muck, there's money'. There are new regulations – many do not think them yet stringent enough – over dumping and tips. There is a Waste Management Paper on recycling issued by government. At last some waste separation plants are appearing. There are plans in some towns for new waste disposal plants, one of which can produce enough energy for a fair-sized town by incinerating rubbish. Although it is rather scandalous that local authorities are not forced to collect rubbish according to contents, it is usually possible to take one's own throwaway glass, plastics, paper, kitchen waste and tins to a central dump where they are collected separately. Some cities, however, are to try out an innovative environmental project which will give recycling a higher public profile, and encourage new approaches, as well as identify the difficulties involved. Sheffield was launched in 1989 as the first Recycling City. Cardiff in Wales, and Dundee in Scotland have followed, and rural Devon has been designated Recycling County. Already the first results of monitoring are to hand. Representatives from industry, central and local government, and the voluntary sector are forming a national working party to oversee what is happening in these selected areas; and each area, of course, will have its working group.

As yet, the heat has not been turned on: this is only the beginning. The situation will force us in the near future to take far more drastic steps. You will remember that in the parable of the Prodigal Son, it was the *situation* that forced him to come to his senses – rather than an interior change of heart. This did not matter, because he went home and his father welcomed him with open arms. Let us all do the same.

PRACTICAL SUGGESTIONS

Meanwhile, there is a lot that we can do individually to help this along. Let me share with you the 5 Rs of recycling, as set out by the Friends of the Earth:

Refuse to be given unnecessary packaging.

Return bottles whenever you can; buy returnable bottles if possible.

Re-use as much as you can. Items such as envelopes, bottles and plastic bags can all be re-used. Take unwanted clothes to a charity shop.

Repair things rather than throw them away.

Recycle paper, cans and bottles by taking them to your local recycling centre. Find out from your local council where this is.

Of course, this is a personal chore – but then all good stewardship involves chores. We must not waste our resources. We owe to God the duty of stewardship. This is not something that just calls for thought: it needs action. Preparing to preach this sermon, at any rate, has tickled my own conscience: it has aroused me to do something practical about our own rubbish. How about yours?

15

PROVIDENCE AND GAIA

*And God said, Let the waters bring forth abundantly . . . Let the
earth bring forth the living creature after his kind.*
GENESIS 1.20, 24 (AV)
*For as the body is one, and hath many members, and all the
members of that one body, being many, are one body . . .*
1 CORINTHIANS 12.12 (AV)

I'm sure that every mother here today, after she was safely delivered
of her baby, said a private prayer of thanksgiving. In the old days she
would have been 'churched' with the Order of Thanksgiving after
Childbirth, but nowadays she is more likely to say thank you pri-
vately. It's not just that the pain and danger of childbirth are over. It's
also because the baby that has been safely delivered has marvellously
developed in her womb so that it can now live in the open air. She now
has complete charge and control over her child, but during those nine
months of pregnancy she had no control whatsoever. Things just took
off under their own momentum. She could influence the baby inside
her for the worse, by smoking or drinking a lot of alcohol; but even
then there were automatic feedback processes which would minimize
the damage. Even if she herself was poorly fed, these same processes
would ensure that her baby did not suffer as she did. Her child had
been kept at a temperature comfortable for life. The baby in her
womb had been given just the right nourishment by means of the cord
which attached it to her body, and had been kept alive by oxygen from
her blood. The various parts of the baby began to form – no one yet
knows quite how – and it grew rapidly. Even the trace elements
needed for healthy living were given to the growing foetus without her
realizing it. A mother feels thankful for all these automatic processes
which were happening for months and months without her conscious
awareness. She senses, perhaps as never before, the providence of
God.

MOTHER EARTH

I take this as an analogy for Mother Earth. I say Mother Earth on purpose, because many Christians would raise their eyebrows at my using such words, thinking of pagan earth worship and such matters. But there it is in the Scriptures. I took as my text those two verses from Genesis, at the beginning of the Bible, when we are told God commanded the oceans and the earth to 'bring forth'. The words 'bring forth' describe the process of birth, of becoming a mother, and their use clearly points to an analogy between birth and creation. There is of course no Great Mother like the Greek earth goddess Gaia, or the Anatolian nature goddess known as Artemis of Ephesus. 'By the word of the Lord were the heavens made.' 'God said, let the oceans and the earth bring forth . . . .' The initiative lay with God.

The analogy of a womb is a very accurate one to describe the whole process of evolving life. In the first place, the oceans and the earth have to be kept at a temperature comfortable for life. The oceans must not exceed a certain degree of saltiness, or no cell could live in them. The air which living things breathe must have the right ingredients in the right kind of mix, so that they can use its oxygen for the basic process of living. And all this happens by automatic processes, complete with feedback. There is no outside interference. Just as a woman looks on what has been happening in her womb as a marvellous example of divine providence, so we also should look on the way in which life has been able to evolve on this planet as another wonderful outworking of providence.

THE BODY AS A LIVING ORGANISM

In fact, the story is even more wonderful than that. When we come to ask how these processes actually take place in the oceans or on earth, we find a kind of co-operation between the various elements. This brings me to my second text about the human body. Paul uses the body to describe the unity of Christians in Christ. He wrote that '. . . the body is one, and hath many members, and all the members of that one body, being many, are one body'. There is a kind of unity in diversity in the human body, and each member has its own function. The foot or the ear or the eye all belong to the body, and have their different functions. I remember once, in the old days when large youth services were possible, I used this passage to explain how young people all had their part to play in the Church. I explained what happened when you cut yourself badly, and the blood poured out: how the clotting agents were summoned, how red corpuscles were rushed to the scene. I realized that perhaps I had been too graphic when I found that girls were fainting away in the gallery! But it's true: we do all belong together in the Church, and we all support and complement one another.

GAIA

The same is true of the earth, or rather let me call it Gaia, because I don't just mean the living things on earth, which are known as biota, but also their whole environment, which we call the biosphere. They make a living unity, and they work together for the good of the whole. The 'Gaia hypothesis' is that the biota and the biosphere together make up a living system which, although many, is one. This living system enables the planet to regulate itself in a way that is comfortable for life. You may be thinking: 'How can inanimate objects, such as rocks, have a part to play within a living organism?' Well, the shell of a snail is very much part of the snail's life, and it couldn't get on without it. As for rocks, when they weather, or lay down carbon, they crucially affect the atmosphere.

You may also be thinking: 'I can see that inanimate things like rocks can have a part to play, but I can't begin to understand how living organisms can help to keep the planet comfortable for life'. But they do. Inanimate processes won't give the fine tuning that is needed. Take the saltiness of the oceans. It must be maintained at 3.4 per cent: if it reached 6 per cent no cell could live in it. Fine tuning is needed to ensure that. Take the climate. The sun has been increasing in luminosity – up to 30 per cent – since life first began on earth; but the climate is kept equable, until we interfere with it. Fine tuning is needed to achieve that. Take the air. Oxygen in the air is maintained at 21 per cent: if it were 25 per cent damp twigs would burn spontaneously: if it dropped to 15 per cent you could not strike a match. Fine tuning is needed for that too. The chemistry is complex; but it is amazing to learn that micro-organisms such as bacteria, and little one-celled microflora with strange names like diatoms and coccolithopores, have a vital part to play in achieving these stable conditions. Bacteria are not bad news but good! Their ceaseless activity in the soil and sediments, in animals and plants, is essential for life. Without their work, you and I could not begin to exist! St Paul used the analogy of the human body in his letter to the Corinthians, and reminded them that 'those members of the body, which we think to be less honourable, upon these we bestow more abundant honour; and our uncomely parts have more abundant comeliness' (1 Corinthians 12.23). It is the same with Gaia. We may think bacteria and other micro-organisms are less honourable, but in fact abundant honour should be bestowed on them for their vital work of keeping the conditions of life stable.

THE PARABLE OF DAISYLAND

If you ask yourself how there can be self-regulatory systems which keep things stable without outside interference, Jim Lovelock, who is the father of the 'Gaia hypothesis', gives us a parable by which to understand it. He asks us to imagine a world like ours, which only has two species of vegetation: black daisies and white daisies. Competition between the two controls the climate, without any outside planning or foresight. The white daisies reflect the heat of the sun back into space, and so cool the earth. The black daisies absorb the heat, and so the earth heats up. If it gets too hot, the black daisies absorb too much heat and die off, and then the planet gets covered with white daisies. But these white daisies cool down the planet, and this enables the right mix of black and white daisies to coexist, which keeps the planet at just the right temperature. If it gets too cold, the white daisies reflect the heat, but can't retain enough to keep themselves alive; and so the black daisies spread, which returns the temperature to normal. All this happens automatically. Multiply this interacting feedback mechanism hundreds of times, and we begin to see how the planet is kept stable within very narrow limits. These mechanisms have evolved of their own accord under the providence of God without which we could not live.

When Jim Lovelock first put forward the 'Gaia hypothesis', it was frowned upon by orthodox scientists, although he himself is a distinguished FRS. They did not like the notion that Gaia is alive, or that organic creatures help to regulate its systems. But he is winning out because his case is solidly argued on scientific grounds which no one can contradict; and he is now beginning to be honoured in the scientific world. It was perhaps unfortunate that he used the word Gaia, the name of a pagan earth goddess, which had been suggested to him by his neighbour William Golding the novelist. His theory is purely scientific. It stands or falls by the way that it fits the scientific facts.

THE PROVIDENCE OF GOD

Gaia helps Christians, I believe, to understand more about the providence of God. I got to know Jim Lovelock by writing to him after reading his book; and I am now President of his Gaia Trust, so I'm committed to the idea. I welcomed Gaia because it chimes in with other signs of the providence of God which scientists have been recovering recently. There is a whole series of remarkable coincidences connected with the 'fine tuning' of the so-called 'constants' of nature, and with the processes of evolution from the Big Bang onwards, without which there would have been no galaxies, no stars, no planets, no life to evolve on earth, and no you or me.

Agnostics and atheists may claim that these are all random chance occurrences; and they go on to say that there is an infinite number of universes and 'failed universes', and among an infinite number, universes like ours, with these remarkable coincidences and with planets like Gaia, are bound to occur. Perhaps; but there can be no proof of any universe other than our own, so their argument only convinces themselves. I am preaching to those who share our Christian faith in God. From this point of view, all these coincidences and the automatic feedback mechanisms and Gaia itself are part of the providential care of God. Of course they evolved naturally, just as the human womb evolved naturally. If we regard the operation of the human womb as an example of divine providence, so too we can look upon the working of Gaia.

A womb is part of a human body which one day will die. In the same way, Gaia came into being shortly after life began, and Gaia will also die, when the climate becomes too hot as the sun reaches the end of its life millions and millions of years in the future. So Gaia is no goddess: she is the creation of God. Nor should we worry that Gaia sounds so feminine. Surely we should rather rejoice at the thought that God said, Let the oceans and the earth 'bring forth' their creatures. The very idea of Gaia makes us realize how interdependent we all are on this earth; but if human beings continue to flout the laws of Gaia needed to keep conditions stable, they are likely to come under divine judgement and die out.

Gaia is becoming sick. Imagine someone you know who has a slight but increasing fever and yet is unable to sweat properly, who develops increasing bruising and peeling of the skin, who has impurities circulating in the blood, becomes more and more constipated and suffers from 'acid stomach'. Would you not think such a person sick? You would not wait until science has *proved* she is sick – you would suggest a doctor straight away. These analogies are not so very far fetched with regard to the present state of Gaia, with her global warming, the destruction of her rain forests, the degradation of her topsoil, plastics and other toxic substances circulating in her oceans, the accumulation of waste substances in her soil in a way that prevents their natural recycling, and acid rain falling on her trees and land. Those who attempt to cure these malfunctions by 'technological fixes' are like people who try to regain health through patent medicines. A doctor might attack each symptom with well-tried remedies. But for true healing a more holistic approach is needed. We need to look not for cures but at the root cause of a sickness; and the root cause of Gaia's sickness is the activity of us human beings. We need repentance, a deep change of attitude. If we cannot reorientate ourselves so that we no longer imperil Gaia's wellbeing, then like some cancerous growth our excision may become needed. This will be brought about by our own actions, resulting in conditions in which our species can no longer flourish. Divine providence acting through Gaia can result in judgement as well as in blessing.

We concentrate so much upon God's revelation in Christ that we forget the providence of God in the world around us. Jesus never forgot it. He constantly taught about the blessings of providence, the love and care of our Father in heaven; and he taught also about its judgements, as in the storm and floods which swept away the house built upon the sand. Gaia recalls us to these wonders of divine providence. Gaia gives us a fresh vision of the wisdom and care with which our Heavenly Father has planned the universe, as well as a warning of what will happen to us if we go on ignoring the natural balances which God in his benevolence has created for his world.

Isaiah, writing centuries and centuries ago, gave us a remarkably apt prophecy of what might happen.

> The earth dries up and withers,
> the whole world withers and grows sick:
> the earth's high places sicken,
> and earth itself is desecrated by the feet of those who live in it,
> because they have broken the laws, disobeyed the statutes and
>   violated the eternal covenant.
> For this a curse has devoured the earth
> and its inhabitants stand aghast.
> For this those who inhabit the earth dwindle
> and only a few men are left. (Isaiah 24.4–6)

It is a terrible warning of what will happen if we go on breaking what Isaiah calls 'the eternal covenant'. The sooner we return to our senses, the better, and respect those divinely ordained balances that keep our planet comfortable for life.

16

GARDENING

*A garden inclosed is my sister, my spouse; a spring shut up, a
fountain sealed. Thy plants are an orchard of pomegranates, with
pleasant fruits; camphire, with spikenard; spikenard and saffron;
calamus and cinnamon, with all trees of frankincense; myrrh and
aloes, with all the chief spices: a fountain of gardens, a well of
living waters, and streams from Lebanon.*

SONG OF SOLOMON 4.12–15 (AV)

You might think that, with a text taken from the Song of Solomon,
my subject is erotic poetry, or, as writers like St Bernard understood
the poem, that it concerns the love of Christ for his Church. If you
think that, I'm afraid that you will be disappointed. In fact, I am
going to speak about gardening, and my text describes an oriental
garden, with water, fruit and spices. It conjures up a delicious picture
of sun and shade, fragrance and blossom, and the background tinkle
of water. It is worth our noticing that when the writer of Solomon's
Song wanted words to describe the seductive beauty of a beloved, he
turned to the imagery of a garden. Earlier he calls her 'the rose of
Sharon, and the lily of the valleys' (Song of Solomon 2.1). Metaphors
from the garden spring naturally to the lips of lovers, because the
garden is a thing of beauty and fragrance, precious and well loved. It
has been so down the ages. The hanging gardens of Babylon were one
of the seven wonders of the ancient world. The Bible ends with a city,
the city of God; but let us not forget that it begins with a garden, the
garden of Eden. That is what the word 'paradise' means in the Greek
language.

OUR NATURAL LOVE OF GARDENS

In Britain people love their gardens. Selling plants for gardens is big
business – you only have to visit a garden centre to see that. In many
European countries people live in high-rise blocks without gardens.
Of course we have many of these in Britain, and that is one of the

reasons why there is such a large demand for cut flowers in a big city. Yet despite this, two out of three houses do have gardens. Sometimes these are large. When I was a diocesan bishop my see house had 3 acres of garden attached to it. It was far and away the best perk of being a bishop, but it was not easy to give it all the attention that it deserved. Most gardens are small. Now that I am retired, our garden measures only 37 feet by 35; but every inch of it is lovingly tended, and this is typical of many such gardens. Why is this?

It is refreshing to be able to renew our contact with nature. Something stirs within us when we see the natural processes of germination and growth. We find the beauty of flowers, plants and trees deeply moving. The variety of their shapes and colours and fragrances delights us. The presence of birds and wildlife is a further source of pleasure – although not the pests like the slugs and greenfly! As we keep down the weeds, we are reminded of their spiritual undertones which we find in the gospel parables.

This love of gardens seems entirely proper. Francis Bacon called it 'the purest of human pleasures'. But it is more than mere pleasure. Gardens speak to us not only of the beauty of creation, but also of the creativity of the Creator. We know that the striking colours of flowers attract bees, which enable plants to propagate their kind; but this does not explain the gracefulness of their shapes or the wonderful harmony of their colouring, or even the marvellous fragrance of some of their flowers or leaves. They are part of the beauty God imprints on his creation. Frances Gurney wrote:

> One is nearer God's Heart in a garden
> Than anywhere else on earth.

I don't think that that is quite true because I am nearer God's Heart when I receive the Blessed Sacrament, but I'm sure you all know what she means by God's presence in a garden.

Because we think of gardens as something very personal, we forget that in the aggregate the gardens of this country cover some 1½ million acres! That is a very considerable amount of land. It constitutes an important habitat for wildlife. I know that wildlife is often encouraged by birdtables and the like, but unfortunately some gardening activities are not in the best interests of the environment as a whole.

THE USE OF PEAT IN GARDENS

Let me speak about one of these. Do you use peat in your garden? Judging from the number of bags of peat sold in garden centres, the odds are that you do. Do you realize that by so doing you are helping to endanger a diminishing national and international resource? Please don't think that this is just the cry of an ecological fanatic. It is endorsed at the highest levels: for example, the use of alternatives to peat actually has government support. Most British peatbogs are located in the north, especially the north of Scotland and, thank goodness, they are too inaccessible for commercial exploitation. It is the so-called Lowland Raised Bogs in England that are under threat. Only about 5,000 hectares of primary bog of this type are now left. It cannot be regenerated. When it's gone, it's gone.

Peat is not a soil nutrient, but it has a great capacity for retaining and releasing water and at the same time for retaining air, which is very useful for some plants. It is also very long lasting if it is not dried out. These are the reasons why people buy it. Surely, you may be thinking, peatbogs are not all that important. But that is not so. They are unique habitats of great importance for wildlife, and for some species their last refuge. They are a valuable genetic source for the future. They act as natural reservoirs of highly purified water, and it is important to retain our wetlands for they have vital ecological functions. Peatbogs are also important for storing and releasing carbon dioxide, although the mechanisms by which they do this are not yet fully understood. If you heed the call not to help in further diminishing peatbogs beyond the stage where they cannot regenerate, then you could easily use alternatives, among which are included bark, coir (coconut fibre) and many, many others. Even with *your* little garden, *you* could in this way help to retain some of our ancient and valuable natural resources.

THE USE OF PESTICIDES IN GARDENS

Do you use pesticides in your garden? It would be surprising if you didn't. Every gardener knows that pest is the right word to describe the insects and wildlife which spoil our growing plants, and the viruses which infect them. Indeed, those who say that all pesticides are wrong are usually not aware of the vast amount of damage that pests can do, not only to plants, but also to food in store, not to mention the 30 per cent loss that pests would inflict on crops if pesticides were not used. But did you know that, quite apart from farmers and professional nurserymen, domestic gardeners spend £30 million each year on pesticides? Some of these are derived from natural sources, such as pyrethrum, and do no lasting harm. Others are very toxic. They linger in the soil. They can affect wildlife, and even human beings. It is the synthetic pesticides and fertilizers of which we should beware. It would be possible for you to avoid using any of these synthetic varieties and to start gardening organically instead. Have you ever thought of that? I am constantly amazed by those people who insist on buying organic vegetables in a supermarket, but who never dream of gardening organically at home!

There are other ways in which we can be 'green gardeners'. We can be careful not to dispose of any toxic substances such as paint and oil by throwing them on the ground. We can make our own fertilizer by creating compost through putting vegetable peelings, grass cuttings and other organic material in a compost heap or compost tumbler. We can plant species that attract wildlife. We can insist on native species of plants and food in our gardens. We can even consider growing some of our own food. These, you may think, are all small matters. Indeed, seeing the size of our gardens, that is true enough. But there are millions and millions of us, and in the aggregate all this adds up to a considerable sum. Furthermore, it can help each one of us to feel that we are doing our bit. When it comes to ecology it is the easiest thing in the world to complain about what others are doing, especially in the world of big business, without in any way changing our own life-style or our own habits.

TRUSTEES FOR GOD

And the earth really does matter. It belongs to God, not to us. We are only trustees for God. This was made perfectly clear by the Old Testament law of jubilee, whereby after 50 years all land returned to its original owner. The earth, like the sea and the rivers and the air, are our primary resources. The topsoil has taken hundreds of years to form: it is an amazing amalgam of living organic matter mixed with trace elements and inorganic substances. We must not spoil it, because it will take a very long time to regenerate. Again, we must not use up valuable and endangered resources like peat. We must not use violent means of killing insects and other pests which result in lasting damage to wildlife and future plant life. The fact that so much good land has already been wasted makes it even more necessary for us to conserve what remains. We owe this to God, and we owe it to those who come after us.

I began by extolling the beauties and pleasures of a garden. I end with a warning, lest in the care of our garden we unwittingly endanger the future. Today is Sunday. The probability is that you will be at leisure for the rest of the day; and no doubt many of you will be out in your gardens. May I ask you to look at them this afternoon as revealing to you something about the creativity of the Creator? And may I also suggest to you that, if necessary, you decide to make some changes in your future gardening practices?

17

ECONOMICS AND ENVIRONMENT

A false balance is abomination to the Lord; but a just weight is his delight.

PROVERBS 11.1 (AV)

Have you ever wondered, when your vegetables were being weighed out at the greengrocer, how accurate the scales were? In fact, it is the task of the local authority to keep a close eye on such matters. In the ancient world there were no such checks. Weights and measures were very important, and overcharging was always possible by using a false balance. The Book of Proverbs roundly declares that all forms of cheating are sinful and hateful to God who loves justice and fair dealing.

UNDERCHARGING FOR RESOURCES

You may well be asking what on earth this has to do with the environment. You may be saying to yourself: 'I don't use a false balance: what on earth is the preacher on about?' Let me tell you. You and I do indeed very frequently use a false balance in the sense that the resources of the earth that we use are falsely weighed. In fact, we are not overcharged, we are undercharged, and we get goods on the cheap. Again, you may well come back at me and ask, 'However can that be? Do we not use the mechanism of the market, a self-correcting device which ensures that the prices we pay go up and down in accordance with supply and demand? For example, when there was a crisis in the Gulf, the price of petrol went up, and when there is a glut, prices tend to come down again.' That of course is true. But the market can only tell us what goods are worth to people now. There are hidden costs of which we are not aware, and for which those who use these resources do not have to pay. If we cause pollution, someone will have to clear it up later.

Surely we can agree that the polluter should pay here and now. It seems a sound moral principle. Why on earth should someone else pay these costs later, quite apart from having to bear the effects of the pollution we have caused until it is cleaned up? And of course the polluter is you and I whenever we buy a pint of milk (whether in its bottle or in its carton), or beer or soft drink in its can. We conveniently forget the cost involved in taking them away to landfill sites and burying them. If we paid for these costs as well, cartons would attract the lowest tax, closely followed by the milk bottle. This is reused on average fourteen times until it gets broken and thrown away.

Or again, take electricity. When we switch it on, we are using coal-burning electricity generators which belch out chemicals which result in acid rain. We ought also to pay the cost of scrubbers which eliminate these noxious gases at source, but we don't, because scrubbers are not being fitted to many of the generating stations. It's a modern equivalent of those false balances which weighed out the wrong costs against which the Book of Proverbs protests. Again, you and I all buy and burn coal or petrol or gas. Once again, we are the polluters, because these cause the emission of noxious gases and of course carbon dioxide, which is a globe-warming gas. Interestingly enough, if we had a tax on fossil fuels (and one of the British political parties has included this in its manifesto at the General Election) we ought to have the greatest tax on coal, because it contains the most sulphur, and the smallest on gas, which is the least polluting.

This raises another point. We only have about a century of reserves for these fossil fuels which power our society. The price of oil, petrol, coal and gas reflects what people are willing to pay for it today. But if we use it today, it will not be available for others later; and when it is in short supply, they will have to be prepared to pay a great deal more for it than we pay now. Think of what they will be saying about you and me! 'Those greedy people who lived at the end of the twentieth century, they wasted those precious fossil fuels at dirt cheap prices, and here are we, paying through the nose for a few gallons when they used to squander thousands and thousands of gallons of the stuff.' This is what they *will* say, unless some other cheap form of energy has been found. That is something on which we cannot count, and which may very probably not happen. This shows how wrong it can be simply to rely on the price of the market now, without adding a tax which will prevent people from wasting these irreplaceable resources. Of course, there are other ways of restricting the use of such resources but, so far as the fossil fuels are concerned, this is much the easiest way.

SUSTAINABLE RESOURCES

What we need to ensure is sustainable development. Development there must be, or how will new houses be built, how will jobs be found for the increasing population of the world, and how will food be produced to feed them? There are some environmentalists who seem to think that it is more important to conserve the natural world as it now is, than it is to attend to the needs of human beings. As Christians we cannot agree, because we believe that human beings are made in the image of God, and must have priority. But we must have the kind of development that is sustainable, and which does not diminish our total capital resources, natural, human or man-made. And yet the kind of development which we now have does just that.

Let me give you an example of what I mean, because it illustrates my text once more: how we use a false balance by which to measure what we are doing. Say you were a citizen of Indonesia. You desperately want better health and education, and more industrial development, because you belong to a developing, non-industrial country. How can you find the money for this investment? What is actually happening is that people are cutting down the tropical rain forests, and transferring their natural capital into human and man-made capital. They seem to be doing well. But in fact they are relying on false balances, which are an abomination to the Lord.

The reason I say this is that if in fact you do what the Indonesians are doing, you are not increasing your capital at all – you are actually diminishing it! For when you have cut down your rain forests, you have lost all the income that they produce: a regular supply of timber, and a host of forest products such as latex, nuts, honey, fruits and so on. The forest removes pollutants from the air, and soaks up carbon dioxide – you will have lost that too. The forest controls flooding, and prevents landslides and erosion and cleans up the water – that is gone too. The forest helps to control the local climate – it will get hotter and crops will be difficult on the cleared land. And of course there are all the people who live in the forest – where will they go and what will become of them? And all the unique species that live in the forest, and all the medical and other uses to which they can be put – all gone too. Instead of a regular income from the capital locked up in the forest, all that remains is some money put to human and man-made capital. Economists who have balanced the books find that Indonesia, far from gaining, has incurred a net loss of capital. 'A false balance is abomination to the Lord.'

But we needn't go as far away as Indonesia. We can look at affairs in Britain. Of course there have to be trade-offs between development and the environment, as I said earlier, or no more houses could be built. How can we decide where they should be built and how much the land should cost? We can find out how much people are willing to pay to keep a view, and we can add that to the charge of the house. But it doesn't really answer anything. In the first place, once the environment is spoiled, it affects not only people here and now, but also people in the future, and it is difficult to put a valuation on that. You might say that it is worth £1,000 to conserve the environment, but the next person who lives in your house might say a quite different amount. And then what about the person who says that the environment is literally priceless, and no valuation of any kind can be put upon it?

VALUES AND VALUATION

We must not confuse valuation and values. Valuation refers to the money you pay for something: value describes its intrinsic worth, which cannot be estimated in cash terms. There are only three ways of proceeding in this impasse. You can either ignore people who say that the environment is priceless, or you can accept what they say and not allow it to be changed, or you can compromise. The most sensible way is to make a judgement in each case which takes into account both values and valuations.

Take a motorway. Complicated sums are done by people at the Ministry. They can put a valuation on time saved, both for leisure and for work, and on accidents prevented. They can put a valuation on the land that is acquired by compulsory purchase, on the noise caused by the cars, and so on. But they can't put a value on the damage to the environment in terms of its intrinsic value. A case occurred lately over the Okehampton motorway in Devon. Dartmoor is a very beautiful area. No amount of argument could persuade a great many people that the intrusion of a motorway was worth the money. Valuations are comparatively easy to handle, but values are quite different. They are God-given. The point was made beautifully in the words attributed to Chief Seattle of the Duwamish-Suquamish and allied Indian tribes in a letter to the President of the USA who had been trying to buy Indian lands:

> How can you buy or sell the sky, the warmth of the land? The idea is strange to us. If we do not own the freshness of the air and the sparkle of the water, how can you buy them?

90

FALSE ECONOMIC ASSUMPTIONS

You may think that it is inappropriate to speak from the pulpit in this way about buying and selling and other money matters. You may feel that economics have no place in religion. But some things do need to be said. It is generally assumed today that economics must have the last word in decision-making and that everything in the last resort can be reduced to financial valuation. This is not so. It is one of the many false assumptions in what is commonly accepted as economic sense today, assumptions that are contrary to those of the Christian faith. Although economics are often said to be value-free, in fact hidden values are usually imported. Everything has its price; we ought to take the most rational decision that gives the most efficient solution to a problem – these ideas are taken for granted by most people today. It is often the case; but not always, as I explained concerning the Oke-hampton motorway.

By contrast, our Christian faith holds intrinsic values as more important than financial valuation. It holds that some things are beyond price. Because the Christian religion is centred on God being made flesh in the coming of our Lord Jesus Christ, it is very concerned with material things, including of course money. That is why false balances are an abomination to the Lord. We must try to see that we do put as correct a price on valuable resources as we can, and that we do our sums right when calculating whether what seems a good investment is really that. But at the end of the day, decision-making about the environment should not be determined by money. We need to make a judgement which includes value as well as valuation.

If you agree with me, then we must be prepared for some very painful changes, both so far as taxes on the use of resources are concerned, and on the decisions we make about the environment.

But then I wonder whether you *do* agree with me, and what action you would be prepared to support if you do?

18
SCIENCE AND TECHNOLOGY

God hath given me certain knowledge of the things that are,
namely, to know how the world was made, and the operations of
the elements: the beginning, ending and midst of the times: the
alterations of the turning of the sun, and the change of seasons: the
circuits of years, and the position of stars: the natures of living
creatures and the furies of wild beasts: the violence of winds and
the reasonings of men, and the virtues of roots: and all such things
as are either secret or manifest, them I know.

WISDOM OF SOLOMON 7.17–20 (AV)

That's a long text, but then science and technology are two huge
subjects. I raise them both today because earlier in this course of
sermons we have been thinking together about the results of modern
technology – global warming, acid rain, fertilizers and pesticides,
nuclear reactors and so on. In some ways I have painted a grim picture
of the effects that these are having on the living systems of the planet.
And this prompts the question: Is technology a bad thing? Would it
not be better for humanity if no advances in technology had been
made? Since technology is the application of scientific knowledge to
practical affairs, a further series of questions is raised. Is science
merely an intellectual discipline which is undertaken to enable us to
impose our will on the world? Is there knowledge that it would be
better for us not to know? Would it have been better if we had not
found out how to split the atom and so achieve nuclear power? Would
it have been better if we had not discovered the secrets of human
generation, and so made possible *in vitro* fertilization of a woman's
ovum by human semen? Would it be better . . . ? The list could go on
and on.

Against this I put my lengthy text from the book of the Wisdom of
Solomon. I know that this book is found in the Apocrypha, and so,
formally speaking, it lacks the authority of being part of the canon of
Holy Scripture as this has been recognized in the formularies of the
Church of England. This is because the Church of England followed
other reformed Churches at the Reformation, and only accepted those

parts of the Bible that had been written in Hebrew; but we did at least say that the Apocrypha could be 'read for edification'. The greater part of Christendom accepts it as part of the Bible. The Wisdom of Solomon was written during the Apostolic Age, and of course in Greek. It naturally betrays a Greek as opposed to a Hebrew attitude of mind, and it gives us an excellent example of the way in which a religious faith can be translated into another culture. I mention this because interest in the secrets of the natural world was not a characteristic of a Palestinian Jew of the first century, but for centuries it had interested the educated Greek mind.

KNOWLEDGE OF GOD'S WORLD

According to my text, Solomon had been initiated into all kinds of scientific knowledge. He was not the only king to be fascinated by such matters: England's own Henry VIII was another. But the sweeping claims that Solomon knew all about astronomy, cosmology, climatology, ethology, botany and all the rest are rhetorical nonsense! Solomon's date was not far off a thousand years before Christ; and it was not until the sixteenth century after Christ that the natural sciences began to 'take off' in the Western world.

But that is not the point of the text, which lies in the statement that all scientific knowledge comes from God: 'God hath given me certain knowledge of the things that are . . .'. All things that come from God must be good. And so there can be no scientific knowledge that in principle is not good for us to know. We may abuse that knowledge: that is another matter altogether. The knowledge itself, because it is knowledge about God's world which comes ultimately from God himself, must be good. Indeed, there are those who claim that the natural sciences could only develop under the attitudes of mind induced by the Christian faith. The creation story in Genesis recounts the regularity of the universe. The Christian concept of contingency requires empirical investigation of the world, not merely logical thought, in order to unravel the laws of nature. The Incarnation of the Word made flesh emphasizes the importance of the material world. Whether or not modern science could have arisen in some other culture is perhaps besides the point. The fact is that it did arise within a Christian culture.

Many people think that the natural sciences are opposed to religious faith. This is partly because of what is now known to be a concerted effort by some scientists in the last century to wrest power and influence from the Established Church, power that they thought rightly belonged to them. In fact, it is manifestly untrue that science and religion are fundamentally opposed. If it were so, it would be inconceivable that some of the most distinguished scientists are deeply religious people. It is true that some of the conclusions of the natural sciences are not easy, as they stand, to square with some of the contents of the Christian faith as we have received these; but scientific conclusions are never final, and the Christian faith can develop in understanding. Gerard Manley Hopkins spoke for all Christians in his memorable line:

The world is charged with the grandeur of God.

The motives of scientists who seek out the secrets of the universe are not readily available to us. Most, I think, have been simply moved by a spirit of curiosity, as well as the feelings of satisfaction at knowing how nature functions. They tell us that there is a real experience of beauty in a good scientific explanation. Other scientists, no doubt, are keen to advance in their chosen career and want to excel. Sometimes the motivation may be to obtain power over nature, but it is seldom acknowledged as such. Such power can only be partial and localized. The interlocking ecosystems of the natural world are far too complex for humanity to 'manage nature'.

TECHNOLOGY IS OFTEN A BLESSING

Technology is the art of harnessing scientific knowledge to practical ends. It goes back to very primitive beginnings, like the invention of the wheel. How can we possibly say that the wheel is a bad thing? Whatever would we do without wheels? Everything transported would have to be carried or pushed! Nowadays, very sophisticated technology is available for most people in the Western world. It so happens that since my retirement I have had to take charge of running the household. I find that the washing machine and the vacuum cleaner make light work of what would otherwise be very heavy chores, while the fridge and the freezer greatly ease the housekeeping. Who could possibly suggest that these are bad things? On the contrary, they are a very great blessing, especially to housewives and retired bishops!

Knowledge that is obtained cannot be unlearnt. Once that knowledge exists, people are bound to use it for practical ends. Medical technology has enabled people to live longer. Mass production of food has enabled vastly increased populations to be fed. Technology through mass production permits multitudes of people to use what in the past only the wealthy could enjoy. It has given us all increased mobility. It has given to many, through medical technology, a new lease of life. It has speeded up and enlarged human communication through the telephone and the mass media. Who of us could possibly wish these to be reversed, even if they could be? Who could even suggest that such uses of technology are contrary to the will of God?

THE ABUSE OF UNDESIRABLE ENDS

Of course, technology can be abused. And of course it is abused. It happens in three ways. It can be used for ends that are undesirable; it can be used in inappropriate ways; and it can be used with bad results which were never foreseen when the particular technology was first introduced.

What do I mean by saying that technology is used for ends that are undesirable? An obvious example is the long-range nuclear missile. Another is the technological expertise that could unleash what is popularly known as 'Star Wars'. Satellites that are useful for detecting forest fires or assessing climatic conditions can also be used for intelligence about an enemy's dispositions. The Allies won the Gulf War so easily because of their amazing intelligence, with some satellite pictures down to a 3-inch definition!The Iraqis, on the other hand, had no idea at all of enemy dispositions. The military in other countries will have realized the vital importance of satellite information in military operations, and they are therefore bound to squander resources in developing sophisticated technology to knock out satellites. We shall even be extending our pollution outside the biosphere! This is an evident abuse of technology, but we cannot expect that it will be outlawed for that reason. Nations have to take precautions for their own defence. The only real way of avoiding war is by means of building up trust and co-operation among the nations.

THE ABUSE OF INAPPROPRIATE TECHNOLOGY

Another reason for regarding these examples as an abuse of technology is the sheer waste of skills and resources. It has often been pointed out that the amount of money even one nuclear submarine costs could fund enormous development schemes in the Third World. These development schemes would themselves involve modern technology, but technology put to a positive use.

This leads us to consider just what is meant by appropriate technology in the Third World. We have all heard of modern hospitals being erected in the bush, replete with all the most modern technology, which the country concerned has neither the money nor the skills to use. (I know we are not using all our hospital beds in Britain, but this is partly because of increased hospital productivity.) What is needed in developing countries is smaller-scale technology which is economical in its use of power and in resources. E. F. Schumacher was the first to point this out with his slogan 'Small is Beautiful'. Western sophisticated technology, which uses large amounts of energy, is usually quite inappropriate. There is inappropriate technology too in our developed world. I might instance such a monstrosity as the electric toothbrush – are most of us really so effete that we cannot muster enough energy to clean our own teeth? Technology is most appropriate when it is both economic to run and most efficient in fulfilling a human need. Modern technology can be more efficient and accurate than human beings – as for example welding by robots in motor manufacture. This will mean less employment in such industries; but there are plenty of other needs remaining to be met which do require employment, and working people will be able to enjoy more leisure.

THE WORST ABUSE OF ALL

The most dangerous technology of all in the long run is that which is introduced to meet human needs, but which by its large-scale use produces effects which were never intended, and which were unthought-of at the time of its introduction. Among these effects we must include acid rain, global warming, soil deterioration, and so on. Some of these can be overcome by better technology. But let us beware of thinking that all our problems can be solved by what is known as the 'technological fix'. Many of them can be; but some world ecological problems will require, especially among the wealthier countries, a radical change of heart and a radical change of life-style if we are to overcome them, as overcome them we must.

A THEOLOGICAL REFLECTION

I would like to end with a theological reflection. God must have known, when he created the universe, that intelligent beings would emerge somewhere or other, as indeed human beings have done on this planet. He must have known that they would use their wits to find out about the world that he had created, and which he inspires with his Holy Spirit. He must have known that these beings would not be content with mere knowledge, but would seek to turn this knowledge to their own practical advantage. He must also have known that if they continued unchecked in their profligate use of resources, they would bring themselves to an untimely end, and in so doing would spoil his own creation. Why then did he create this kind of world? We cannot answer for God. But we can perhaps suggest that God's creation has enabled us to evolve as free and responsible beings, able to make our own decisions which will affect our future. He puts such great weight on freedom. He deliberately faces us with the requirement of voluntary self-restraint.

Can you and I and the whole human race measure up to that challenge?

19

MATTER AND MATERIALISM

A man's life consisteth not in the abundance of things which
he possesseth.
LUKE 12.15 (AV)

According to St Luke, Jesus prefixed these words to a parable which
has a striking parallel today. A farmer prospered greatly, and his
barns could not hold all that the earth brought forth. He said: 'This
will I do. I will pull down my barns, and build greater; and there will I
bestow all my fruits and my goods' (Luke 12.18). But God said to
him: 'Thou fool, this night thy soul shall be required of thee: then
whose shall those things be, which thou hast provided?' (Luke 12.20).
Today's parallel to this concerns not an individual farmer, but the
Common Agricultural Policy of the European Community. Storage
facilities for grain put into 'intervention stocks' (as the jargon goes)
are greatly overstrained. Did you know that in Ireland there are no
barns left, and the grain has to be stored in the holds of ships?

GROSS NATIONAL PRODUCT AND THE HUMAN
DEVELOPMENT INDEX

Well, you might say, this is a mere temporary aberration until the
policy is corrected. If only it were! The whole basis of modern economics is to produce more and to sell more and to consume more. The
philosophy on which its theory is based is known as 'utilitarianism';
that is to say, people will be more and more happy the more and more
they can get. And people grow very worried about economics. Britain
seems to be for ever taking its economic temperature. People become
upset when the percentage of goods manufactured drops only a deci-
mal point or two. We are always hearing those three letters GNP,
which stand for Gross National Product; and unless GNP is going up,
our morale tends to go down. We tend to judge the whole state of the
nation by the percentage increase of 'growth' compared with last year!
'Growth' never means spiritual growth, or cultural growth, or any

98

other kind of growth other than economic growth – that is to say, growth in material wealth. How often do you hear anyone admitting that they are content with what they have, and grateful to God for what they can buy with it? No, we are always wanting more money so that we can buy more things. Why else over the last ten years have we insisted that average incomes should have risen far faster than inflation?

As a matter of fact, there *is* a growing awareness that our quality of life does not necessarily increase with our standard of living: otherwise people wouldn't be so worried about our environment. The United Nations is aware of the situation; the officers of its Development Programme have constructed a fascinating table, which compares what it calls its 'Human Development Index' with GNP per head. They are very different. GNP per head shows income per head, while the HDI, or Human Development Index, combines standards of literacy with life expectancy (which gives an indication of health). Now you might think that those countries which are materially most wealthy would have the highest standards of education and health. But you would be wrong. For example, the USA has the highest GNP per capita, but it ranks only nineteenth in the Human Development Index! The Netherlands, which is only no. 14 in the GNP ratings, comes fourth in HDI – that is, in health and education. Great Britain comes only eighteenth in the GNP ratings, but it is right up in tenth place so far as health and education are concerned.

Health and education are both very important, and they contribute considerably to human fulfilment. Who among us would prefer to have more possessions at the expense of our health and our education? Would you prefer to be materially wealthy with a short life, or an educated person in good health? Of course, you might think, I would like both material wealth and health and education; but if you can't have it all, which would you prefer? I presume, from the very fact that you are in church today, that you would have heeded Jesus' words, and you would prefer to rank high in the HDI table rather than the GNP table. But Jesus' words were not particularly concerned with either health or education. I am sure that he would have said that what above all is important is our relationship with God and our relationship with our neighbours. After all, he told us that the whole moral law depends on the command to love God with all we possess, and our neighbour as ourselves.

And yet we are surrounded on all sides by the demand that we pile up more and more possessions and consume more and more 'goodies'. This is the common assumption of fiction and drama. Beguiling advertisements in the mass media urge us to buy this or buy that, and

99

we are hardly even conscious of the inducements – sexual among others – which are employed to help to persuade us. Jesus said in the passage from which my text is taken: 'Take heed. Beware of covetousness'; but covetousness is just the attitude of mind which advertisers hope to induce in our acquisitive society.

MATERIALISM AND THE ENVIRONMENT

This of course has bad effects on our spiritual health, but this is not what I want to emphasize now. I want to stress how it produces a market for ever-increasing production of goods. It means that more and more raw materials are used, some of them non-renewable. It means that more and more energy is required to make this increasing number of goods, with the result that more and more carbon dioxide is released into the world, and factories and electricity-generating stations produce more ingredients for acid rain. It encourages us to consume more and more food and drink. This may well adversely affect our health, but I am not concerned with that now. I *am* concerned that it will mean more and more energy used up in providing fertilizers and pesticides to enable the food to reach us, and, so far as beef is concerned, it means more cattle are farmed, and more methane gas released into the atmosphere. It means more and more lorries are required to deal with increasing freight, which release more polluting gases into the air. And so I could go on. I haven't even mentioned the wastes that consumer society produces. Jesus said: 'A man's life does not consist in the abundance of the things which he possesses'. I want to add that the more abundance we each possess, the more we are stripping the planet of non-renewable resources and increasing pollution globally. Of course, this need not necessarily be the case, if we were to adopt sensible and stringent measures of pollution control and recycling; what I *am* saying is that as things stand today, this is what in fact is happening.

MATTER AND MATERIALISM

The attitude of mind which regards possessions as the most important things in life we call materialism. Jesus condemned it unreservedly. But this does not mean that material things are to be condemned in themselves. On the contrary, the Christian religion puts an enormous

100

emphasis on matter. God created the material universe, and 'behold it is very good'. You and I are human beings who are made up of material substances. We express ourselves in physical ways, through speech, by the way we look, and by many non-verbal means of communication. We are creatures of the earth: we love to run the soil through our fingers or to dangle them in water. We like the feel of the wind, the tang of the sea, the smell of the rain. We enjoy our food, and we believe that the pleasure which we experience through the physical act of sex in marriage is God-given. We human beings are very material; and Christianity is the most material of all religions. For we use matter for actions that bring us very close to God: water in baptism and bread and wine in the Holy Communion. What could be more material than these? We call them 'sacraments' because they are outward and visible signs of an inward and spiritual grace given to us.

Would you not agree with me that even more important to us than sacraments is the person of Jesus himself? And he was very material. We believe that he was fully a man as well as fully God incarnate in matter. 'And was incarnate by the Holy Ghost of the Virgin Mary, and was made man' – how often have we said that in the Creed? And we know that it lies at the very heart of our faith. And just because of our belief in the importance of matter, we are concerned with the right use of material things, and with the processes that produce them as well as the people who make them. Matter is important to us not only for its intrinsic worth, but also because God created it. It is also important because of what it expresses and means, and because of the use to which it is put.

And that brings us back to the environment. The environment is, above all, material. It concerns our material surroundings in the biosphere. It concerns all other living things who live in it. The matter of which the environment consists is important because of what it is in itself, for its intrinsic value, and also because of the use to which we put it. Do we use it sensibly or selfishly? Do we use it thoughtfully or thoughtlessly? Do we use it wastefully, or with respect and consideration for others? These are the questions which our Christian beliefs about matter force us to ask ourselves.

Finally, as we compare matter with materialism, we find an absolute contrast between the two. Materialism, the belief that matter is the only reality, and that the more we have of it the better, is a false faith utterly repudiated by our Christian principles. On the other hand, matter, created by God, is worthy of our greatest respect, because it has intrinsic value, and the way in which we use it expresses our intentions and our values. Jesus said: 'A man's life does not consist in the abundance of things which he possesses'. He never said

101

that possessions are bad. He never said that we should not possess anything of our own. What he did say is that our life does not consist in the abundance of things that we own. Such a belief in possessions is not only death to us spiritually; but, carried to its logical conclusion, it would also bring death to those who come after us through a depleted and polluted planet. The various environmental crises we now face are caused by a deep-seated malaise of the planet, located in the only form of being which is capable of free will – that is, the human race. Unless the whole human race can repent and re-orient its goals, it will by its technology harnessed to human greed bring upon itself divine judgement. Like the man who built bigger barns, its life will be required. 'A man's life consisteth not in the abundance of things which he possesseth' – but your life and mine does consist in the abundance of good relationships we have with others, and above all with God.

How do we stand there?

20

THE CHURCH AND THE ENVIRONMENT

And unto this people thou shalt say, Thus saith the Lord; Behold, I
set before you the way of life, and the way of death.
JEREMIAH 21.8 (AV)

'It's up to you: the choice is yours.' So said Jeremiah in 588 BC to Jews
besieged in their capital city of Jerusalem by the Chaldeans who came
from what today is Iraq, and he was putting before them the choice of
staying there and dying or leaving the city and falling into the hands of
the Chaldeans. Neither alternative was pleasant; but the first meant
death and the second meant life.

THE ROLE OF A PROPHET

Jeremiah was a prophet, and it is the task of the prophet to 'forthtell'
the truth, unpleasant though it may be, and by so doing to call people
to repentance. It was agony for Jeremiah to have to do this, and of
course he found himself in trouble. At one stage he was left to die in
the mud at the bottom of a dungeon. But he was rescued, and continued to say what he had to say, because he knew it was a word from
the Lord.

Our situation is just the same today. The future of the planet is up
to us. The choice is in our hands. We can either moderate our ways,
and ensure that posterity will be able to live comfortably on the earth,
or we can go on as we are going on, and then the future will be death.
Neither of the alternatives is pleasant. We don't like having to change
our ways, and we don't like endangering our future; but, as with
Jeremiah, one means life and the other means death. It is the task of a
prophet in the Church to say this, and to go on saying it. He must not
expect the message to be popular, and he will not necessarily expect
that it will be heeded. But if he believes that it is a word from the
Lord, then he must go on saying what he has to say. There have not
been many talking in this way about the environment from within the
Christian Church – in fact, in the past there have been far more

outside it than in it. But there have been a few. Barbara Ward, a great laywoman who died, alas, early of cancer, was one of them. Ernst Schumacher was another. The point I want to make is that prophecy is the calling given by God to individuals, and it is seldom if ever given to the whole Church. It is an extra blessing when this gift is given to one of the Church's leaders, but they are not chosen as prophets to the world, but as leaders of the Church.

BOOKS AND POETRY

This is not the only way that individual Christians can make their mark over matters such as the environment. Another way is obviously the writing of books or appearances in the mass media. Another way, rare but remarkably effective, is by poetry. Have we not, many of us, been moved when we have read St Francis of Assisi's 'Canticle of the Creatures', with its invocations to Brother Sun and Sister Moon, Brothers Wind and Air, Sister Water and Brother Fire? Listen also to these lines about conservation by that great religious poet Gerard Manley Hopkins:

> O if we but knew what we do
>> When we delve or hew –
> Hack and rack the growing green!
>> Since country is so tender
> To touch, her being so slender,
> That like this sleek and seeing ball
> But a prick will make no eye at all,
> Where we, even when we mean
>> To mend her we end her,
>> When we hew or delve:
> Aftercomers cannot guess the beauty been.
> Ten or twelve, only ten or twelve
>> Strokes of havoc dissolve
>> The sweet especial scene,
>> Rural scene, a rural scene,
>> Sweet especial rural scene.

It is, I fear, given to even fewer people to be great poets than it is to be great prophets.

A FALSE WAY FOR THE CHURCH

If the Church is not prophetic and certainly not poetic, what is its function in matters of the environment? Should it offer solutions to environmental problems? Sometimes it is tempted to do this. For example, the World Council of Churches staged a World Convocation on Justice, Peace and the Integrity of the Environment in Seoul in 1990. The Roman Catholic Church was invited to be a co-invitee to the Convocation, but, although there were Roman Catholics present, their Church felt that it could not co-sponsor the occasion 'because the Catholic Church and the World Council of Churches are by nature two different bodies'. (I mention this because it is sad that the Churches cannot even co-operate to help save the planet. The ecumenical movement still has a long way to go!) At this Seoul Convocation, approval was given to a fossil fuel tax. This may well be a good thing; but it is not the task of the Church to suggest particular remedies for ills. Had the Roman Catholic Church been officially represented, it might well have prevented such a foolish recommendation by a Church convocation. For the Church does not have the expertise to do this: how can it know which is the best measure to take among many options? It is not the task of the Church to make precise and politically sensitive proposals.

'MIDDLE AXIOMS'

What then should the Church be doing? It should help its members – you and me – to understand the seriousness of the environmental crisis. It should clarify both the theological reasons for this, and the moral imperative which underlies action which must be taken, majoring on stewardship. It may also include what are sometimes called 'middle axioms' – that is to say, demands which stand half way between the moral demands which we find in the gospels, and the realities of the actual situation in which we find ourselves. These middle axioms will, however, not embrace measures of policy, but only the moral imperatives of our present situation. An example of such a middle axiom is that 'We have no right to spoil the planet for those who come after us' and 'We must take steps to prevent global warming, with the catastrophe which would accompany it'. We must leave it to others to decide what particular action to take.

THE CHURCHES' RECORD

You may not be surprised to hear that the Church has not distinguished itself in matters of the environment. The Orthodox Church, which had in the past the best theological understanding of the environment, has said nothing, since it is not accustomed to speaking out on secular matters. Regretfully, in the Roman Catholic Church Cardinal Ratzinger, its chief authority on doctrinal matters, has spoken against the Green Movement! But very late in the day, in 1988, Pope John Paul II, in his Encyclical on the social concern of the Church, does mention environmental matters in discussing development – but it is contained in just one paragraph out of a total of 49, and contains no sense of the gravity of our present situation. Other churches have done better; for example, the Dutch Reformed Church has involved itself fully in such matters, which is one reason why in the Netherlands stringent environmental regulations are in force. In England in the more recent past, some cathedrals, Canterbury and Salisbury among others, have held Festivals of Creation, and these have made some impact. But right back in 1970 there was an attempt to bring these matters before the Church of England, by the publication of a report for discussion, followed by two further reports in later years. The Archbishop of Canterbury then invited a group of theologians to reflect on the theology of the environment, and their report was published in 1975. But its impact was minimal. Have you, I wonder, ever heard of this report called *Man and Nature*? I am sure you haven't. I fear that the same must be said of the actions taken by Councils of Churches. For example, the British Council of Churches staged public hearings on the proposed nuclear breeder reactor, and the World Council of Churches on nuclear power generally – but, once again, I am sure you haven't heard of them. It is a fact of life that few people take much notice of what Councils of Churches say or write! It is a pity that the Churches should have such apparently little influence, because it is only by understanding that we are accountable to God for what we do to our planet that we are likely to find the moral and spiritual resources to put things right.

THE CHURCH AND OTHER FAITHS

You might think that all faiths could work together in this matter. Indeed, I used to think so myself. Although our beliefs are very different, we all have a deep respect for the environment. The Jewish and Christian tradition is that of stewardship. In the Muslim tradition, man is God's *kalifah* or deputy, from which it follows that man must be responsible for the environment. Hindus and Buddhists believe in reincarnation and this gives them a very practical reason for respecting the animal creation!

It would seem that they should be able to work together. But I have been persuaded that it is better if different faiths each concern themselves with their own members, since it is very difficult to co-ordinate them all, and it would be unlikely that agreement could be reached. The World Wide Fund for Nature, to celebrate its 25th birthday, gathered together at Assisi representatives of the five mainstream faiths in 1986, and each issued a statement on the attitude of their faith to the natural world; and this has been followed up by many groups in many countries. This was a splendid initiative, and we can only hope that they will issue a joint statement, each to the members of his own faith, about the gravity of the situation before the great UN Conference meets in Brazil in 1992.

WHAT CAN WE DO?

All this, however, seems somewhat remote from your and my level of church participation. What can we do as Christian men and women? How can we not only do something ourselves, but help to influence other people? I think that we should join the many secular environmental organizations and make our contribution in them as Christians. If we want definite guidelines for this, perhaps I may share with you an Environmental Ten Commandments which I first suggested way back in 1972, but which I see no reason to change nearly twenty years later:

I am the Lord your God: you shall have no other gods but me.

You shall not make to yourself any graven image or idol, such as GNP or possessions or riches, whether in the heavens above, or in the earth beneath, or in the waters under the earth: you shall not bow down and serve them.

You shall not take the name of the Lord your God in vain by calling on his name, but ignoring his natural law.

Remember that you set apart one day in the week for true festivity, or you will be bored stiff in the technological age you are bringing on yourselves.

Honour your father and mother, but do not seek to prolong their term of life so that they are miserable.

You shall not murder future generations by your present greed.

You shall not commit sexual sin by producing more children than is your right.

You shall not steal the inheritance of posterity.

You shall not bear false witness against your overseas neighbours by lying to yourself about the extent of their need.

You shall not covet an ever-increasing standard of living.

You may remember that when we use the Ten Commandments in the liturgy of Holy Communion, we end by saying together, as we might well say now: *Lord have mercy upon us, and write all these thy laws in our hearts we beseech thee.*

21

INTERNATIONAL ACTION

*And [God] hath made of one blood all nations of men for to dwell
on all the face of the earth . . .*

ACTS 17.26 (AV)

These are the words Paul is reported to have said in Athens on Mars
Hill. It is one of the few occasions described in the book of the Acts of
the Apostles when he was speaking not to Jews but to pagans. He
therefore appealed to their natural sense of God, which was in those
days a universal characteristic; and in so doing he emphasized the
unity of mankind. It is a theme found very sparingly in the New
Testament. Paul does indeed write trenchantly in the epistle to the
Romans about the solidarity of all people in sin, but in his speech at
Athens his emphasis is different: he is speaking of the unity of all
nations in as much as they derive from a common ancestor. Whether
or not we did all derive from a common ancestor – a matter much
debated among anthropologists – none of us doubts today the unity of
mankind. We all share a common humanity. We are all bound
together by the common bonds of this humanity. Today this feeling is
reinforced for you and for me in two ways. In the first place we are
haunted by that picture of earth which those astronauts saw from their
spaceship on their way to the moon – nothing could make it clearer
than that that we all have a common home. And secondly, the media
bring before our eyes every night in the television news pictures of
humanity from all parts of the globe; and, as was the case in the recent
attempt by a Russian junta to take over the government of the USSR,
we see history actually unfolding before our eyes. This forges a link
with our fellow human beings in other parts of the world whom we
can both hear and see as they speak and act. We feel a bond with them
all.

IS INTERNATIONAL CO-OPERATION REALLY FEASIBLE?

In matters concerning the environment, it is clear that action needs to be co-ordinated not only at a national level, but also internationally. Pollution, such as acid rain or nuclear radiation, does not stop at national boundaries. Unless there is co-ordination between the nations on matters affecting the whole planet – say the loss of the ozone layer or global warning – no action that any one nation takes can be effective. It is of little value one nation adding an environmental tax to the price of some substance which, if used, will increase world pollution unless other nations do the same: otherwise the nations which do not add the tax will be at a very unfair advantage in the manufacture, and thus in the export, of their goods. International agreement and international action are badly needed.

Yet we must ask whether these are really feasible. Human beings suffer from original sin; and human societies such as states or countries tend to be inherently self-regarding. We are not totally corrupt: God forbid. There is real goodness in us still, and states are capable at times of real generosity when their people are deeply moved, as can be seen at critical times of famine when massive help is given by states as well as by individuals. However, I am not talking about such critical moments: I am talking about what is needed, so far as we can see, for the indefinite future of humanity. Is it not part of our Christian teaching that a person needs to be reborn in Christ in order to be re-oriented in a proper relationship to God and to his or her neighbours? Is it not part of our experience too that even Christians who claim to be reborn in this way may still be selfish and self-regarding? Do we not find this same self-regardingness from time to time within the institutional Church as a whole? How, then, can we expect unregenerate societies, consisting for the most part of those who are not Christians, to behave towards one another in ways which subordinate their own selfish advantage to the common good? It is often assumed in the secular world that if only the right kind of organization can be found, world co-operation could be easily secured. Nothing could be further from the truth. We need to accept the fact that the unregenerate human is inherently selfish.

There is, however, one way in which genuine co-operation, which we have seen to be vital for the future of the planet, may be properly secured. Archbishop William Temple once wrote as follows:

It may be the function of the Church to lead people to a purely disinterested virtue (though this is at least debatable); a statesman

110

who believes that a mass of citizens can be governed without appeal to self-interest is living in dreamland and is a public menace. The art of government in fact is the art of so ordering life that self-interest prompts what justice demands.

What applies to you and me as citizens of our country applies all the more to the various countries of the world in their search for international agreement.

It is therefore a top priority for environmentalists to show politicians that it really is a matter of self-interest for all countries to co-operate for the common good. However, environmental measures often take a long time to make themselves felt, and environmental dangers often lie in the future rather than the present; in contrast, politicians, if only because their terms of office are usually limited, tend to take only a short-term view. But ordinary people like you and me – that is different. We are concerned for the welfare of our children and grandchildren. It is therefore vital not only to alert politicians to dangers, but above all to alert ordinary people as well, so that they can make their views known. Politicians then have to take note, because they are dependent on votes for their re-election.

WHAT HAS BEEN ALREADY ACHIEVED

In fact, an enormous amount has already been done. When I first interested myself in ecological matters way back at the end of the 1960s, I was regarded as a freak. But the United Nations held its Conference on the Environment in 1972, preceded by Barbara Ward's best-selling paperback, *Only One Earth*. This made a tremendous impact on public opinion worldwide: the environmental movement took off, and it has never looked back. Until the Gulf War and the recession, surveys in Britain showed it to be people's major concern. In 1990, 52 per cent said that the environment will affect the way that they vote, and 58 per cent said that they would prefer to live in a country which emphasizes the environment more than living standards.

There have even been some successes worldwide, or almost world-wide – for example, over the protection of the ozone layer, when, a few years ago, at the Montreal Convention and in subsequent additions to the Convention, the majority of nations agreed to phase out the main ozone-depleting gases. But even here we need to be alert. The rich countries promised to spend £240 million helping to buy

111

poor countries ozone-safe technology. India alone estimates that it will need £1.2 billion to comply with the ozone treaty. By the end of 1991 the fund contained merely £9 million. (Earlier in 1979, at the United Nations Conference on Science and Technology for Development, the rich countries promised £250 million, of which less than a third has actually been given.) Nonetheless, some things have been achieved. The OECD countries – the rich ones – have adopted a code of environmental conduct. The European Community has pledged to stabilize carbon dioxide levels at 1990 levels by the year 2000, and to go on cutting them 'substantially' thereafter. Its Council of Ministers has even suggested the imposition of an energy tax to help to curtail carbon dioxide emissions.

THE UNITED NATIONS CONFERENCE IN BRAZIL IN 1992

As of now, plans are afoot for another UN Conference on the Environment and on Development in Brazil in 1992, popularly known as the 'Earth Summit'. Great hopes are being placed on it – perhaps too great. It is hoped that an 'Earth Charter' of environmental and economic principles will be agreed, and that the nations will subscribe to what is called 'Agenda 21', a document which will set out a long list of different targets and schedules for solving particular problems. It is hoped to agree worldwide firm targets for reducing emissions of carbon dioxide, the chief global warming gas. It is hoped too there will be international agreements on protecting biological diversity, on tropical forests, and on ways of transferring clean technologies to poor countries so that they can continue their economic growth without damaging the environment. That is a very large agenda, and it is unlikely that all these hopes will be fulfilled. For example, there is a real problem about the reduction of carbon dioxide and methane. The planet could never support a population of 10 billion people emitting carbon at the rate of Western Europe today, which would raise such emissions to four times their present rates. But to restrict the carbon emissions of developing countries would be to prevent their economic development. An Indian report on the environment comments on global warming: 'Behind the global rules and global discipline that is being thrust upon the helpless Third World, there is precious little global sharing or even an effort by the West to understand the perspectives of the other two-thirds'. In any case, at present the USA, the biggest polluter by carbon dioxide, resolutely refuses to agree to limit its emissions, and the Chief of Staff at the White House did not even

112

believe that there is any problem of global warming at all. (He has since resigned.) Indonesia, which plans a vast increase in its pulp and paper industry from cutting down its rain forests, threatens to boycott the Conference, if there is pressure put on it to curtail its felling of trees in order to solve a problem caused not by Indonesia, but by the wealthy countries. Perhaps these difficulties will have been solved before the Conference, but others are bound to arise. We cannot hope to achieve unanimity 'at the drop of a hat'. The importance of the Conference, it seems to me, lies in the extent to which it can arouse public opinion worldwide, and *initiate* (rather than perfect) a new era of international co-operation between governments.

A CHALLENGE FOR US ALL

There seems little that you or I can do when it comes to international co-operation; we are not involved as individuals. It is governments that matter. It is not only the British government that matters, but co-operation between the governments of the world. But we should not be without hope. If things have already moved so fast, can they not continue to do so? God must have known that a crisis of this kind would arise, when he determined on a cosmos where intelligent life would evolve; and, as St Paul reminds us in the first epistle to the Corinthians, 'God is faithful, who will not suffer you to be tempted above that ye are able, but will with the temptation also make a way to escape' (1 Corinthians 10.13).

Some things we can all do. We can support pressure which could help our government to play its full part in these matters. And we also all have a work of prayer to do, both for the Conference itself, and all that flows from it. Will you play your part in this? The future of the planet is at stake.

22

THE KINGDOM OF GOD

*But seek ye first the kingdom of God, and his righteousness; and all
these things shall be added unto you.*

MATTHEW 6.33 (AV)

What a comforting text this must seem to any of you who feel com-
placent about our environment! Put God first and all will be well, it
seems to say. It comes from the Sermon on the Mount. Jesus has said:
'. . . take no thought, saying, What shall we eat? or, What shall we
drink? or, Wherewithal shall we be clothed? . . . For your heavenly
Father knoweth that ye have need of all these things' (Matthew
6.31–32). And Jesus follows my text with the words: 'Take therefore
no thought for the morrow: for the morrow shall take thought for the
things of itself . . .' (Matthew 6.34).

Perhaps you will say to me: 'What do you make of that passage?
You environmentalists are always taking thought for tomorrow – you
are always on about what will happen to the planet if we continue as
we are. You are always on about what we shall eat, when you talk
about population outstripping world food production. And you do ask
"What shall we drink?" because you go on about the quality of drinking water, and pesticides and fertilizers leaching into the soil and
then into the water table. Again, you ask "Wherewithal shall we be
clothed?" when you go on about the energy and resources taken up by
the manufacturing industries.' And perhaps you may end up with a
real body blow. 'The trouble with you environmentalists is that you
don't take the gospel of Jesus really seriously!'

Well, we will see about that. First, let us look again for a moment at
that passage in the Sermon on the Mount, and see what it really
means. When the Authorized Version has 'take therefore no thought
for the morrow' it is translating the Greek verb *merimnate*. This does
not mean 'don't think about'. It means 'don't get worried about', and
that is very different. We are not to get worried about food or drink or
clothes or tomorrow. And of course, as always, Jesus gives us the
advice that we need. Worry never helps anyone. Worry never makes
anyone better. It only clouds our judgement, and worse still, it fixates

114

our attention on the matters which concern us so that we forget about God. As Jesus said: 'Is not the life more than meat, and the body than raiment?' (Matthew 6.25). However important environmental matters are – and in this course of sermons I have suggested that they are very important – they are not the most important thing in life. The most important thing is our life with God.

JESUS AND THE KINGDOM

Even if you accept that this gives us the real meaning of the passage, I expect some of you may have been thinking that environmental matters have been given an exaggerated importance in these addresses. Most of my texts have come from the Old Testament, not the New. Little enough has been said about the teaching of Jesus, and nothing at all about his saving death and resurrection. Acid rain and global warming and the ozone layer may be very important; but surely in the pulpit the preacher should address the great themes of our salvation and redemption? Should he not speak about grace and forgiveness and reconciliation with God?

Well, of course he should speak about such things; but I would not have dared to preach on these themes unless I believed that they are entirely appropriate for a Christian pulpit. And I want to demonstrate this by taking as my text today, at the culmination of this series, the very words of Jesus, 'But seek ye first the kingdom of God, and his righteousness; and all these things shall be added unto you'.

The good news of Jesus – and the word 'gospel' is simply Anglo-Saxon for 'good news' – is about the Kingdom of God. St Mark's gospel tells us that at the beginning of his ministry, Jesus came into Galilee, preaching the good news of the Kingdom and saying, 'The time is fulfilled, and the kingdom of God is at hand: repent ye, and believe the gospel' (Mark 1.15). And we have to ask ourselves: What does he mean by the words 'Kingdom of God'? Jesus never answers that question directly. He tells us what it is like, by his wonderful parables: it is like the seed growing secretly, it is like a dragnet, it is like a grain of mustard seed, like leaven, like a lost coin, and so on. In this way he gives us an imaginative insight into the effect that the Kingdom has on us, or the attitudes we need in order to enter into the Kingdom. He doesn't actually tell us what it is.

However, he has no need to do so. We tend to forget what the words 'Kingdom of God' actually mean in their ordinary literal sense. They mean the kingly rule of God, his kingship over the whole of life

– not only over our own hearts, but over the whole of the society in which we live. That is what the Kingdom of God is about. Jesus himself is the Christ not because he talks about the Kingdom, but because he is the Bearer of the Kingdom; he brings it by his own presence. Wherever he is, we are brought up in his life against the kingly rule of his heavenly Father. We are brought face to face with God himself. He embodies in his person the Kingdom of God because he is perfectly obedient to his heavenly Father in everything he says and does. He speaks of the Kingdom drawing near, as if it were just round the corner during his lifetime, casting its shadow before it comes in his own life. He speaks in this anticipatory way because it was not until his death and resurrection that Jesus completed the task of bringing us into the Kingdom and enabling us to share it with him. Through these events of our salvation we are enabled to be identified with him, and so to be more obedient in our lives to the kingly rule of God.

THE ENVIRONMENT AND THE KINGDOM

But this does not mean that in this life as it stands we do not have any glimpses of the Kingdom of God. Certainly, this is only for those with eyes to see, because these signs are hidden from public view. One of the ways in which God exercises his kingly rule is by his providential ordering of our world. We have seen many ways in which this happens. The sun is at the right temperature, comfortable for life. The ozone layer prevents it from harming us with its rays. There is a wonderful system of recycling trace metals which we need for our health. The sea is kept at the right saline mixture. The air cleanses itself naturally, and oxygen is renewed by a complex system by which chlorophyll in the green things enables plants to absorb carbon and transpire oxygen. Water is recycled by evaporation from the oceans into the skies, and falls again as rain on the earth. We have food to eat, water to drink, and shelter and clothes with which to protect ourselves. The list of God's providential care could go on and on. It is part of his kingly rule on this planet. So it is part of the Kingdom of God; but only for those who have eyes to see. From others it is hidden, because they only look on it as the way things naturally happen in accordance with the mechanisms and laws which natural science has uncovered.

If we keep the natural law, if we do not tinker with these natural mechanisms which God in his providence has arranged to evolve on earth, then it is true that all these things – sufficient to eat and to drink and to be clothed – will indeed be added unto us. If we seek first the Kingdom of God in the natural world and the right working of nature ('his righteousness'), these good things will be our inheritance. But if we interfere with these natural mechanisms which are part of God's kingly rule, then things will not go well with us. Again, if we act like good stewards of creation, we shall not waste our non-renewable resources, and then indeed it will be true that we need not be anxious about the morrow, because there will be sufficient; and tomorrow can worry about its own troubles.

There is a further point here. There can be no big improvement in the state of the world environment without peaceful coexistence between countries and within countries, and unless rich countries exercise self-control in the use of non-renewable resources and are willing to export new technologies, and poor countries are released from enslavement by huge debts owed to the wealthy countries. Reform is also needed in the Third World over land tenure and unrestricted capitalism (or communism) if sustainable development is to be promoted. These themes are beyond the scope of these sermons; but I mention them here because they involve peace and justice, and peace and justice, like respect for the environment, are essential elements of God's Kingdom here on earth.

THE KINGDOM OF GOD, PRESENT AND FUTURE

I hope therefore that I have shown you that preaching about the environment is one form of preaching the Kingdom of God. Of course it is not the only form. Far from it. Preaching the Kingdom also includes preaching about our forms of relationship with one another in the world of people, so that these may be brought under the kingly rule of God. It also involves preaching about the need to bring all our institutions and the life of society under the kingly rule of God. Above all, it means inviting people to put their trust and confidence in Jesus Christ the Son of God as bearer of the Kingdom, so that when we open our hearts to him and identify with him, and when we are brought by him face to face with God, our lives are reoriented, and we ourselves are brought more fully under God's kingly rule.

Of course, in this life none of this happens perfectly. We are frail and fallible creatures, wayward and self-willed, constantly swayed by feelings and impulses which make us miss the mark; and so our obedience to God's kingly rule, even when we live our lives in Christ, is very imperfect. This is why St Paul said that flesh and blood cannot inherit the Kingdom of God. He meant that the completed Kingdom, when God is perfectly acknowledged as King, and thus when he exercises his kingly rule without any human disobedience, cannot lie in this world, but in the world to come.

IMITATING GOD IN HIS KINGDOM

But here and now we do live in this world, and it is up to us to see that we leave this world in no worse a state than we found it. Indeed, we should do more than that. If we are to be godlike in our actions, then we must imitate God who is our creator, redeemer and sanctifier. We must be creative in using our knowledge to adapt the world of nature to our needs without endangering it – for example, by using biotechnology to make the seeds we need for our food pest-resistant and disease-resistant. That would indeed be using our creative gifts in God's world. Or again, we must try to put right those aspects of the environment which others before us have spoilt. That would indeed be helping to redeem the natural world. And we must recognize the intrinsic worth of all of creation: the rocks, the air, the bacteria, all living creatures great and small. God's Holy Spirit is in all creation. That will indeed be our way of helping to sanctify the creation. We are to be co-creators with God, co-redeemers and co-sanctifiers. I do not mean by that we are in any way putting ourselves on, or anywhere near, the same level as God – simply that we are trying to be godlike in the way in which we act towards the creation, as befits those who are made in the image of God.

It lies within our power to do this. If we make up our minds to do so, we can help to create the environment, heal the environment, and respect the environment. This is a great and noble task set before us. But it is not the most important task that God gives us. Our most important work is to respond to God's love with our own, to worship him, and to enjoy him for ever.

To him be glory for ever. Amen.